CLOSE ENCOUNTERS

CLOSE ENCOUNTERS

CHRISTIE BLATCHFORD

KEY PORTER BOOKS

Canadian Cataloguing in Publication Data

Blatchford, Christie
Close encounters

ISBN 1-55013-096-X

1. Canadian wit and humor (English).* I. Title.

PS8375.B74 1988 C818′.5402 C88-094275-4
PN6178.C3B56 1988

Key Porter Books Limited
70 The Esplanade
Toronto, Ontario
Canada M5E 1R2

Design: Marie Bartholomew

Phototypesetting: Computer Composition of Canada, Inc.

Printed and Bound in Canada

88 89 90 91 92 6 5 4 3 2 1

This, as the late Mama Cass once sang, is dedicated to the one(s) I love, especially my husband, my mother, and my good friend Marcy. Oh, and my dog.

Contents

PART THREE: BREAD AND BUTTER

PART FOUR: PROFESSIONAL HELP

PART FIVE: FRIENDLY FIRE

By Way of Explanation

I am thirty-seven years old.

I know more adults than kids with full braces on their teeth. I'm not sure what this means, but it makes me nervous. How the hell can I be expected to talk seriously to a high-powered executive whom I would have called Metal Mouth on the playground? Though I am no longer young and by some standards, though certainly not my own, am approaching middle age, I am not old; yet I remember when it was children who wore the braces.

I remember:

—when the great majority of people got married and stayed married and died married, and all to the same person. There were no Congratulations-On-Your-Divorce cards or court battles for custody of Sasha and Leroy, the Lhasa apsos. "Ex" was just another prefix, not the world's tallest free-standing prefix to a former spouse.

—when "nanny" was a term of endearment for a grandmother, not the stranger who raises your kids. Children had one last name and were not known as Bennett-Jones, Brenda, or Jones-Bennett, Brenda, depending upon which parent's weekend it was. "Daycare" didn't exist as a word let alone as a rallying cry.

—when a person was not assigned an employment-termination counsellor, she was given the boot. No one had mentors, only well-placed relatives and in-laws; companies paid their people to work, not to quit smoking or lose weight.

—when masturbation was the course of last resort, not celebrated as a viable safe-sex option; celibacy was aspired to only by the clergy, with limited success. People were afraid of the dark, not of commitment; therapy was for a bum knee, not a vocation; middle-aged men got the hots for girls, but felt no compulsion to describe this perfectly understandable state as mid-life crisis.

—when most people went through life without ever hiring a

contractor or interior designer; there were no ads, on milk cartons or in bus shelters, for missing children; and you would have assumed a "serial killer" was someone who knocked off the entire box of Cheerios.

—I admit it. These sound like the ramblings of someone who belongs in a rocking chair, an old broad who passes the day on the porch of her Retirement Village (called "Golden Fronds" or "Sandy Vista" and located hard-by a twelve-lane expressway and an outlet mall), her watery blue eyes clouding over as, with her walker, she shuffles down memory lane to The Good Old Days, when life was simpler.

But Lord thundering Jesus, those are my ramblings, and I have lived for just thirty-seven years. For maybe twenty of them have I noticed such things (until you pass adolescence, you notice only what you see in the mirror). All of this suggests that maybe life really was simpler in The Good Old Days and, worse, that things change so fast that The Good Old Days may have been last week.

And nothing changes more or more quickly than the intricacies of our assorted relationships. For, I remember (here she goes again!) when there were family, friends, and acquaintances. And that was pretty much it.

Now the average Joe often has a handful of parents (the originals and post-divorce replacements — not to mention, the adopted child's new social imperative to bond with his Birth Mother), several families (children and ex-in-laws from a first marriage; more children and new in-laws from the second), several sets of friends (His, Hers, Theirs, who come with more exes, part-time children, new lovers), a deck or two of acquaintances (those he works with, those she works with), and a battery of professionals (psychiatrists, therapists, counsellors) and service people (nannies, daycare teachers, mother's helpers, gardeners, babysitters, renovators, lawyers, real estate agents, caterers) whose collective job it is to make life as simple as it would have been naturally twenty years earlier.

When my own father, who died two years ago, turned

seventy or thereabouts, he rebelled against all of the above. "I don't need any more friends. I don't want any more friends." He would meet someone new at his office, run into the effervescent newest spouse of an old pal, or my mother would try to cajole him into going to a party. "Jesus Christ," he'd always say, "I have enough friends. I don't want to know anyone new."

He could get away with it; he was of an age when eccentricity is not only accommodated, but expected. He was retired from full-time work and not climbing career ladders; besides, he was old enough to have had some wonderful relationships, and at least one of them, with his wife, was still going on. He reacted to change (or, more precisely, to the changing nature of relationships) by telling it to fuck off.

Most of us can't or won't do that.

We need to know how to get along with bureaucrats, because if we don't, they'll get us; we have to be pleasant to the lovers and spouses of our friends because we want to keep our friends. We must grasp the fundamentals of office politics if our careers are not to stall; if we pound the living daylights out of the smug administrator of our kid's daycare center who charges us $10 a minute after five o'clock, she'll dump our kid and phone one of the desperate parents on her waiting list. Besides, lots of us are just plain lonely. All in all, we meet and form relationships with more people in a year than our parents may have known in a lifetime. And the world not only gets more complex, but smaller, a fact that will not have escaped you when trying to avoid a former spouse or someone you fired. So, we must either get along with or be tolerant of most of these folks.

It may still be true that you makes your bed, you lies in it; but it is also true that, now, there are likely to be a great many people in it with you.

I am convinced that the trick is to turn yourself into a human version of the infamous and mythical Wampus Bird. He, when pursued, flies at ever-increasing speeds in ever-decreasing circles until he disappears up his own asshole, from which point of vantage he laughs gleefully at his baffled pursuers.

Alas, by the time most of us recognize the wisdom of this course of action, we're too old and stiff to perform the necessary acrobatics. Thus, this book.

PART ONE: Blood

The Nest as Featherbed

It is a genuine modern phenomenon, duly noticed and analyzed in our daily newspapers and rendered numbingly mundane by its frequent discussion on the talk-show circuit. Yet the bottom-line questions remain: Why are so many older teenagers and young adults still living at home? And what the heck can their parents do about it?

Unlike so many other so-called trends — which mean the same half-dozen people exert their influence on their friends in the media to have publicly declared "hot" such diverse things as Balloon Skirts and Personal Fitness Trainers and Tofu — this one seems to have spread into the real world. Many of the young adults I know, most of them in their early twenties, most from relentlessly average families, are still living at home and show no signs of wanting to do otherwise. A good number of those who have left learned that the world can be both disagreeable and prohibitively expensive. They have returned to the nest, not with their tails between their legs, but rather cavalierly.

This is a great switch from the sixties and seventies, whose teenage products were chomping at the bit to move out and get their own apartments, not to mention the freedom to stay up all night. Most of my friends left the parental home at eighteen or so; the few who stayed much longer were regarded with suspicion. Even my brother's generation, those who grew up in the late forties and early fifties, wasted no time in getting out; and before that, the Second World War provided a kick in the pants to young men, if not young women.

Over time, it came to be deemed normal that young adults feel the need to get out on their own at an early age: no wonder all those parents who grew up believing this are disconcerted to find that this generation has reverted to the ways of centuries past. Then you had two choices: (a) you lived at home until you got married, which is why, not coincidentally, people married so bleeding young, all parties concerned being frantic for some privacy; or (b) if you were female, overweight, overprotected and, therefore, unmarriageable you were not expected to leave, ever. (What's the point, if you aren't going to be A Wife And Mother.)

Frankly, I haven't a clue why this is happening, and don't much care; my concern is with the poor, befuddled parents who are seeing their dreams of an empty nest (with all its joys — the bath to themselves; the chance to watch television without hearing, in the background, the steady thump-thump-thump of a bass guitar; the opportunity to make love on the couch) systematically destroyed. Let the sociologists, who have already come up with such implausible explanations as The State of the Economy and The High Cost of Housing, figure out what's going on with the young; after all, in terms of experience, mental acuity, and emotional range, the two groups are much of an age.

Fortunately, there are a number of things desperate parents can do to prompt their elderly child to pack his old kit bag. Some of these may be unpleasant evocations of Tough Love (a pseudo-trend that could be described as You Only Hit the Ones You Love). But they work.

1. Under no circumstances should parents do an elderly live-in child's laundry, or make his bed, or clean his room. If, heretofore, they have been so foolish as to offer the personal services that are impossible to find even in good hotels, they should cease and desist immediately. Elderly children very often stay in the home because it is ever-so-much easier to do so; parents who behave like chambermaids deserve what they get.

2. As the elderly child refuses to do the grown-up thing and leave, parents should attempt to treat him as they did when he was a genuine child. Demanding of a twenty-five-year-old with a full beard that he pass around the hors d'oeuvres at parents' parties or perform ("Do the monkey call, Henry") for the guests may be sufficiently humiliating to induce an overdue exit — and not, I hasten to add, merely from the party.

3. Impose a curfew, even if the elderly child has never before had one. Say such things as, "If you're going to live in this house, you'll have to abide by our rules" and then ground him Monday to Friday. Ask if he has finished his homework yet. It is my belief that modern young adults are unwilling to move out because they are the products of overly liberal parents, who have always allowed them to do whatever they liked and whose childraising philosophy was, Use Your Own Judgment. Why should a twenty-three-year-old woman bother leaving her parents' home if her boyfriends have been sleeping over since she was sixteen? Act like a parent, even if it is fifteen years too late.

4. Ask the elderly child to pay a reasonable rent. Parents may rightly ask where else could the child find a private, one-bedroom apartment for $150 a month? Parents who feel particularly guilty about doing this should point out that, being terribly old (which all parents are to their children), they must put away something for their retirement.

5. Parents who have tried all the above, and still find themselves sharing their home with an overgrown elderly child, should consider putting the house up for sale. (Often

the mere threat is enough to get the child moving.) This worked very well with a family I know: Due to Financial Reverses, these parents did need to sell their rambling four-bedroom home, but you can imagine their relief when, just as the house was put on the market, their elderly child (a twenty-two-year-old with a full-time job, a full-time man, and a bank account bigger than either of her parents') announced that she had found a place of her own, and the parents were able to buy the small, two-bedroom bungalow they craved.

One of the newer variations of a tired old cliché is, "When I was ten years old, my parents moved. It took me two weeks to find them." As with all clichés, there's a measure of truth and wisdom in this one, and parents with resistant elderly children should remember it. After all, though there are organizations to trace missing children and animals, there is, blessedly, no such thing as Parent Find. Yet.

The Birth Mother Syndrome

People have been adopting children, probably, for as long as there have been children, which is to say, nine months to the day after Eve took a bite of the old apple. Probably, too, adoptees have always had a certain curiosity about their roots — particularly about why their biological parents gave them up. (I know I would be curious; I would also be a tad peeved.) And probably, adoptive parents have always found it a little awkward to break the "Honey, I'm not really your mum" news.

Still and all, it has never before been a recognized rite of passage for an adopted person to burn with Birth Mother fever; never before have there been groups and associations lobbying for the cause; and surely, never before has the phrase, "Well, I'm adopted, you know" been regarded as an automatic badge of suffering — or, for that matter, offered up as an excuse for rude behavior.

I remember, as a child, hearing that So-and-So was adopted; I was told that it meant that So-and-So's parents chose him, and that he was rather special, and doubly wanted, because of it. I distinctly remember wondering, when I was annoyed with my parents, why I hadn't been lucky enough to have been picked out by some real winners, instead of kept by the cruel beasts who had had me. And despite what you hear now from the pop psychologists about the torment that being adopted can bring a child (in the form of schoolyard taunts and the like), I don't buy it. I mean, like most kids, I was both a tauntee and a taunter in the schoolyard: as the former, I was either Fatty Fatty Two By Four or Fred (for Fred Flintstone, to whom I bore a unfortunate resemblance); as the latter, my remarks encompassed physical weakness (Four Eyes, Skinny, Ugly) and what I considered wittier, personal slurs ("Laura stinks", "Sharon is a slut", "Alex is a crybaby"). But I tell you, I never once heard anyone chant "Andy is adopted, Andy is adopted", and I bet you didn't either.

Now, however, legions of adoptees regularly take out ads in the classified columns of newspapers, appear on radio and television shows, hire private dicks, and generally spend vast amounts of time, energy, and money to trace their "natural" mothers.

This done, they then take out more ads, and spend more money, to arrange a meeting with the Birth Mothers, who show up because they already feel guilty about the whole thing. Thus, all over North America uneasy twosomes, who haven't seen each other in twenty-three or thirty-five or forty-six years, are meeting at the best tables in trendy restaurants. (No one trendy enough to fall prey to Birth Mother Syndrome would eat in a regular hamburger joint.) Over a meal of artfully arranged foreign lettuce, the natural mothers are then obliged to pour out the Whole Sordid Tale (usually, they were just ordinary pregnant teenagers who gave up the babies they were barely older than), snitch on the natural fathers, and, begging forgiveness, embrace their long-lost children.

If the mothers are lucky, this is where it will end; if not, they will be guilted into maintaining an ongoing relationship — usually more lunches in trendy restaurants, such being the trendy adoptee's idea of what is meaningful and important — even if, as is likely, the Birth Mothers live with families of their own three thousand miles away.

Meanwhile, adoptive parents have to endure listening to their kids on talk shows blabbing the whole story; suddenly getting used to being called by their first names by their children, who now address the stranger-cum-Birth Mother as "Mom". This is the thanks they get for driving the kid to ballet school or the hockey rink? For walking the floor with the little bugger when he/she had colic for six years? For explaining that acne is not terminal?

Put in the very best light, it is appalling manners on the part of the adoptees. Certainly, it is tiresome. And, more than anything, it is absolutely unnecessary: I mean, if it ain't broke, don't fix it, right?

Caught In-Between

When I was a small child and deeply into toilet-type humor, I used to delight in loudly pointing out to my parents anyone who had what we called a "Caught-be". This was short for "caught in-between", and referred to someone whose underpants (or jeans or whatever) had ridden up and become visibly trapped between the cheeks of his/her ass. "Mommy, mommy," I would screech in my high child's voice, "that lady has a Caught-be!"

As I usually performed the trick in public places, it became one of those family legends that parents endlessly repeat to their kids once they are fully grown. You know the sort of thing: My husband's mother, for instance, is forever telling the story of How David Got Drunk at Fifteen, Passed Out on the Front Lawn, and Nearly Froze to Death. I have heard that story at least as often as my husband has heard about my Caught-be routine.

But I digress: I describe the original meaning of Caught-be only so you will understand why I think it is such a perfect description of so many people of my generation, who find themselves responsible for two entirely different sets of people — their children and their parents — who are in it, as it were, up to their asses.

Given that our parents are living longer than previous generations, and that we are having our children later in life than previous generations did, it was probably inevitable that, on the same day, you may find yourself trying to get your toddler into daycare and your mother into a retirement home, with all the attendant tugs on your heart, and the guilt.

I can think of a half-dozen friends who fit the Caught-be mold:

There's the woman, nearing forty, who has two children under the age of six and a part-time job — and is subject to the sometimes querulous demands of her widowed mother, who can't pick wallpaper for her dining room (which the daughter would put up) or decide whether she will move from her house (a sale the daughter would handle). There's the woman who was torn between moving house and new baby to Miami (where her husband had a fabulous job opportunity) and knowing that, if she did, she'd be leaving her ailing, eighty-year-old father alone. Then there's the middle-aged couple struggling with the meat-and-potatoes crises of their teenagers' lives and nursing two sets of ill, elderly parents. And there are countless others out there, trying to strike a balance between arranging birthday parties and doctors' appointments for their kids and anniversary bashes and doctors' appointments for their parents.

So widespread is the Caught-be situation that in most

major North American cities, there are now experts who lead Caught-be support groups and run Caught-be workshops, usually with warm titles, such as, "Caring For the Elderly Parent". (Of course there are experts and support groups and workshops for every problem, including imagined ones, so this is not necessarily significant. But more on that later.)

However, without minimizing the very real dilemma of the Caught-be's (I, too, have my hands full, striking a balance between the demands of my dog, who needs to be walked, and my mother, who likes to be driven), it strikes me that past generations might be green with envy — and not only because having grandparents around usually means a built-in babysitter. Anyone who has lost a parent prematurely (and it always feels premature, let me tell you) will know whereof I speak. My friend with the two kids under six and the mother who makes her crazy says that sometimes she feels like she's everyone's mommy, including her mother's; given the lousy alternative, however, she'll make do, thanks very much.

Family Law(s)

1. No matter how different they think they look, no matter how different they may have looked once, and no matter how much they may wish to look different, all daughters eventually end up the spitting images of their mothers. You may safely remark on this resemblance to the mothers, who, being considerably older, will be pleased as punch. Tell it to the daughters at your peril. To wit: "Gosh, you look just like your mum."

"No, I don't. Everyone tells me I look like my dad [blatant lie]."

"You're kidding. You look exactly like your mum."

"No, I don't."

"You don't have to get hostile, Sarah. I meant it as a compliment."

"Fuck you."

2. No kitchen in the world is big enough for a woman and her mother-in-law. No matter how the woman has arranged hers (say, she washes the dishes in the left sink, rinses in the right; bread in the breadbox; J Cloth left in a ball), her mother-in-law will have arranged hers in exactly the opposite fashion (wash in the right sink, rinse in the left; bread in the fridge; J Cloth precision-folded, like an army-cot sheet).

3. Women with older sisters have no difficulty treating them as they do everyone else in the family, which is to say, sometimes with disdain; men with older brothers worship them all their lives. This has nothing to do with the fact that the older brothers may have beaten them up with astonishing regularity. What it has to do with is that the older brothers let the younger ones play hockey with them even when they could barely skate. Well, that's what I think; what I know for sure is that a man's older brother is untouchable, and everyone should remember it.

4. At some point in your life (most often, when you have children of your own), you will become obsessed with your family history. Unless you want to end up writing away to one of those Rent-a-Tartan joints (which, ha, ha, "trace" your roots and purport to discover that you, and everyone else who pays $30, is a direct descendant of Bonnie Prince Charlie), you would do well to pay attention when your parents and/or aging relatives talk about how Great-Grandpa Ernie met Marge.

5. Black sheep vary from family to family, but they tend to fall into at least one of the following categories: they have not married, and are old enough to have done so several times; they have no children, and are old enough to have grandchildren; they are gay; they are more interesting than the rest of the family.

Why People Have Children

My mother-in-law's name is Lorraine. I have known and enjoyed her for seven years, downright loved her for much of that time. Never once have I been able to call her by name. I can swear like a trooper — any old and inventive new Anglo-Saxon curses regularly fall from my lips — but I am incapable of saying the L word.

In the early years, I occasionally addressed her as Mrs. R. and referred to her as "David's mum". Most of the time, I settled for a long, and, I hoped, affectionate "Hiiiii" (in person) or "It's yoooou" (on the phone). As our relationship warmed up, these terms seemed too cool and detached; I searched frantically for an alternative: "Mum" wouldn't do (I had one already; she was one already); I considered, and rejected, "Lor" (too contrived), "Newf" (which she is, but as I already have a friend called Newf, she would have to be Newf Jr. or Newf II, which seemed unfair), and "Rutherford" (it is her last name, but unless we began playing pickup hockey together, it sounds forced). Back to "Hiiiii" and "It's yoooou". I regarded as a great victory when, in the course of writing her a letter, I managed to type "Dear Lorraine".

Then one day, we were visiting the parental home, surrounded by my brothers-in-laws' and sisters-in-laws' various and sundry children. Suddenly my ears perked up. Here was a daughter-in-law talking about "Gramma"; there was a son-in-law using the same word. Then it hit me: The reason people have children is to have a comfortable handle for their in-laws.

Menagerie à Trois

When I was a child, I had two extremely odd and irritating habits. One was that, instead of cuddling my dolls, I would grab them by the hair and bang them against the nearest wall until, in my twisted version of Let's Pretend, I heard them scream, and stopped. (I did this, incidentally, at the behest of my rotten old father, who taught me the trick. That I took to it so quickly was all my doing.) The second was that when I played Mommy, and took my doll's carriage out for a stroll, I did not do it with a doll therein. I dressed one of my cats in my doll's clothes (complete with bonnet) and wrapped blankets, strangulation-style, tight enough 'round the chin to render it immobile. All the old ladies (well, they seemed old then; they were about the age I am at this moment) who lived on my street, on passing me by, would say, "Oh my, what do you have in there, Mrs. B?", look deep into the carriage, and screech in horror when their eyes found not a smiling plastic face, but the furious, spitting one of my cat.

On the surface of it, my sordid past would seem to disqualify me from further comment on the subjects of kids and pets; but, in fact, I quite like members of both groups, though I have no trouble telling them apart. This is more than I can say for some folks, which brings me to the point — the pet as child. Increasing numbers of modern couples appear to regard pets and kids as an either-or proposition (in fact, they go together quite nicely). Not surprisingly, many opt for the pet. This would be merely curious if it ended there; alas, it often doesn't. Some of these couples proceed to treat the pet as they would a baby. I know several such couples, one of which has turned the lower level of their giant house into — you guessed it — not a family room, but a "dog room", in truth a whole floor where the rabbit-like furballs they own can run free. The other two couples, being less affluent, content themselves with buying huge and unnecessary amounts of costly apparel for their dogs.

I am the last person who would begrudge a human being the comfort and love of animals (being the current mistress of three cats and a large black hound); but I would, in the interests of accuracy, like to point out the ways in which pets, especially dogs, are not like children, and the reasons why they should not be treated as such.

1. If a child relieves itself in public, it will do so discreetly, in its diaper, and no one (unless he ventures too close) will know the difference. In any case, no one will insist that you change the diaper immediately. A dog makes a great Broadway-style production of the matter, complete with much circling, digging, sniffing, and squatting before he swings his rear quarters, often damp and rocked with flatulence, into the faces of passersby. Everyone will know precisely what is going on, and, should you fail to clean up the mess, will tell you about it. Score one for the child.

2. Even male infants, who may later grow vast quantities of hair on their backs, require protective clothing. This is expensive, especially if the child lives in label-conscious urban areas, where a baby's first word is likely to be "Roots" (or, as babies are wont to pronounce it, "Wootsths".) Dogs come with hair, and unless one is talking about taking a Chihuahua to Moose Factory for the winter, they never need clothing. Score one for the dog.

3. Both dogs and children require walking. Dogs, however, will do it at your convenience, say, at noon, and are quite agreeable to doing it out of doors. They will also walk on their own. Children demand to be walked at ungodly hours, confining you to the house — or worse, to the halls of the house — and, until they reach a certain age, must be carried while you do the walking. Score one for the dog.

4. Pets do not speak English. There is thus no pressure to send them to French immersion, so they can impress their friends by speaking English 99.9 percent of the time, only lapsing into French while touring Provence on expensive field trips with their high schools. (For the record, my feeling about French immersion is this: It is no different from throwing the kid in a lake. He may learn how to swim, but he'll never like it.) Score another one for the dog.

5. A properly trained dog is welcome in more places than a properly trained child. This is not necessarily right, but it is true. Score one for the dog.

By my count, the dog wins, four to one.

I understand why so many folks are opting for a dog. What I fail to grasp is why they then treat the pet like a child, and burden themselves with the guilts and responsibilities that go with having children. The moral is, if you have a pet, you are not required to carry about its picture in your wallet. Neither should you: it is the adult equivalent of putting your cat in a dress and strapping it into a stroller.

Big Nurse

It happened to a friend of mine when her son (a beautiful, but precocious little devil) was all of eight. They were at a park, fooling around on the playground equipment. "Mom," said her boy, as she was on her way up the ladder to the top of the slide, "be careful. Hold on to the sides when you come down." "I know," she said, "how to do it." A few moments later, the wind having picked up, he said: "Do up your coat, Mom. It's getting cold."

She recognized it immediately, of course, because it had already happened to her and her mother — role reversal, that strange game of topsy-turvy that happens to every parent and every child. Suddenly the child is worrying herself sick about the parent catching a chill, or slipping on the ice, or, God forbid, not eating right.

It hasn't happened yet between my mother and me (though I do fret when she picks at her breakfast), probably because she is reasonably hale and hearty; but it did happen with my father, especially after he became sick. I took great pains to hide it (though I didn't fool him for a second, which is no doubt why his last affectionate nickname for me was Big Nurse), but from the moment his emphysema was diagnosed until he died, some eight years later, from lung cancer, I worried for and about him the way he certainly did when I was a child.

In my most subtle way (which is akin to being beaten over the head with a sledgehammer), I would inquire, in machine-gun fashion, what he'd eaten that day, if it tasted good, if he'd had his medicine, how his breathing was, if the heat (cold/wind/rain) was getting to him, if he'd gone for his walk and done his exercises, how work had been, if he'd watched the news and what he'd thought (I figured if he was still interested in and argumentative about things, he was fine), and where he and my mother wanted to go for breakfast that Sunday (thereby assuring him that he would be around that long). I did this at least once a day, sometimes more often, and though it probably drove him crazy, he never let it show — because he knew why I was doing it: I loved him.

It was exhausting and terrifying watching him grow old (and grow away), just as it is for a parent to watch a child grow up (and also away). The most awful part was the realization that I couldn't make him safe, which is to say, well. I only realized this when he died, and a dear friend of mine wrote me a long and lovely letter. She had the same close relationship with her father that I did with mine. When her dad had died a few years earlier, she said it was as though she'd been fearing and dreading that day for much of her adult life. Now that it had come and gone, she knew she'd never, ever again worry so much. It can happen only once, she wrote.

I'm not sure though: My mother took a bad fall on the ice one winter not so long ago, and I could feel it all coming back — the fear, the fretting, the overwhelming wish to lock her in a room where nothing could hurt her. Big Nurse has not gone away, she is just in the shadows, waiting. They say there is nothing worse than a parent to outlive her child, but I wonder: When the parent and the child change places, as they invariably do when one gets older and more frail, is it any easier? I think not.

Dirty Laundry, Then and Now

1960s	1980s
— teenage pregnancy	— daughter who has first baby at age forty
— shotgun marriage	— child in third marriage
— child living in sin	— child living with four roommates of opposite sex
— marrying someone of a different race or religion	— marrying someone of a different sex
— twenty-five-year-old son marrying fourteen-year-old girl	— twenty-five-year-old daughter marrying eighteen-year-old boy
— finding condoms in son's wallet	— not finding condoms in son's wallet
— child busted for using drugs	— child busted for drinking and driving
— going in son's closet and finding *Playboys* there	— going in son's closet and finding son there
— alcoholic relative	— fat relative

Buddies

I always get the statistics mixed up with those for cancer (I can never remember if it's one in ten or one in five, or which is for which) and I'd bet, if you asked some of the families involved what their first reactions were, they'd admit (sheepishly, I hope) that at the moment of truth, they might have opted for the latter.

I refer, of course, to what used to be called The Love That Dares Not Speak Its Name. Plenty of gay men and women may be shouting that name from the rooftops now, but for lots of them, breaking it to the folks is still another matter. And yet the odds, whatever they are, seem increasingly good that a modern family will have to come to grips with a gay son, or a gay daughter, or a gay brother, or a gay father. As one not very subtle comic put it, "For a group that isn't supposed to be able to reproduce, there sure are a lot of them around". The truth is that for every homosexual who came out of the closet during the Gay Liberation movement of the seventies, there's another one who heads straight back in the second he walks through his parents' door.

Of all the gay people I know, only a handful aren't hiding their sexuality from the family — and only then because their parents are dead. For just about all the rest, their homosexuality is still a secret, if only at home.

It's like that for Sean: The product of a traditional Irish Catholic home, he is, in all the ways that matter, a wonderful son. A successful caterer, a well-adjusted and extraordinarily kind, loving man, he's a volunteer with the local AIDS committee and has been such a sterling, selfless "Buddy" to several gay men dying of AIDS that he undoubtedly prolonged both the length and quality of their lives. He is, in short, the kind of human being parents dream their kids will turn out to be.

But Sean has long since given up the idea of telling his parents the truth: The last time he went home to Ireland, exhausted from months of round-the-clock nursing of his latest AIDS-stricken "Buddy" and near the brink of collapse, he tried to broach the subject — not of his own gayness, but of his volunteer work with People With Aids (PWA). Really, he just wanted someone to talk to, to find a little release. His mother and father, he says, froze him out; they didn't want to talk about "those homosexuals" even in an impersonal, unthreatening way. Sean was not surprised (he had tried before to work his way up to such a discussion) but he was very disappointed.

His "Buddy" at that time was Alex, a young American-born product of the wildest days of sexual liberation, almost a caricature of the promiscuous gay man. Sean had come out late in life, after a marriage gone wrong; Alex knew, even as a young teenager, that he was gay, and never bothered to hide it. Sean has had only a few lovers, each in a long-term, monogamous relationship; Alex had had hundreds. Sean feels wicked if he has the odd joint at a party; Alex regularly shot cocaine into his arm, shared needles, and spent half his salary on drugs. (The rest went on *Harper's Bazaar, G.Q.*, all the fashion magazines.) "Sex, drugs, and rock 'n' roll? — Well no," says Sean, "it was worse than that. It was sex, drugs, and disco. He didn't even like good music."

Had Alex not been felled by AIDS, Sean says, they never would have met. "He was the kind of gay man I hate; he represented everything about gay men that I hate — the drugs, the bars, sex in the bushes. Alex really would have brought out the homophobic side of me."

But they did meet, and became friends, and then good, loving friends. At the end, Sean was everything to the forty-year-old man in the wasted body — his eyes (Alex went blind, as many PWAS do), his ears, his legs, his advocate, his lawyer, his nurse, his hand-holder.

Alex's family, who had always known he was gay, were there for him, too: His mother and sister came up from the States to visit; his bedridden father wrote him daily, loving letters; his nieces and nephews rallied 'round. So he was gay — he was still their Number-One son, their baby, and they were at his side at his death. He was Alex, he was theirs, and they all loved him — unconditionally.

Alex was, for much of his life, silly and superficial. Sean says, "He took a wrong turn in the road. Had he run with the hare instead of the hounds, he would have been a lovely man." In the final months, that's precisely what he turned out to be. One of the last things he said to Sean was, "Why couldn't I have loved someone like you?"

And the sad part is that Sean — kind and sensitive, intelligent, capable of immense commitment to everyone and everything he touches — is a stranger in his parents' home. Because he's gay. You would think more of us would know that what we do in bed is such a tiny part of what and who we are.

Widow Ladies

A few months after my father died, I decided, rather arbitrarily, that it would be a Good Thing if my mother, who was terribly lonely, came to live with me and my husband. As we were then living in the world's smallest house (it was really a large bachelor apartment with a basement), this meant selling it and buying a new, larger place. Over dinner, I broached the subject to my mother. I was, I admit, at my persuasive best: She would have her own apartment in the house (but we could have meals together once in a while); she would have privacy (but we would always be there); she could keep her crabby old cat (and occasionally babysit our dog); etc., etc.

I sold her on the idea, and almost the next day, put our tiny house on the market and went in search of another. After the house had been listed less than twenty-four hours, my mother announced that she did not want to move in with us. We couldn't afford to buy in her neighborhood, she reminded us, and she'd miss all the faces she knew — the women in her apartment building, the cashier at Dominion, the superintendent, even the surly folks with whom she fought regularly at the post office. At first (well, not just at first — for a few months), I was deeply hurt and more than a little outraged:

There I'd been, the Dutiful Daughter, and there she was, rejecting my grand scheme.

Some considerable time has passed since then, and though I remain unconvinced that my mother was right, I can now acknowledge that she may have had a point — and more to the point, that I didn't, and don't, necessarily know what's best for her. It has done nothing, however, to ease my fears about the future, and what will happen if she can no longer manage a place of her own.

Nursing homes do nothing for me. I accept them as a necessary evil, but would rather see my mother in jail than in one of them. (For one thing, the food is probably better in jail, and at least you can smoke in your cell.) One of my grandmothers spent her last years in such a home. It was one of the best of its kind: in a good area, prohibitively expensive, and with all the bells and whistles — fancy dining room (where everyone dressed for dinner); meals in bed if you wanted them; nurses and doctors on the premises; large, lush suites big enough for much of my grandmother's heavy, dark furniture. I visited her there several times, and came away depressed every time: A rose is a rose is a rose, and a nursing home is a nursing home is a nursing home — cold, institutional, and patronizing — no matter how much it costs.

At the other end of the economic scale there are places like the one where an acquaintance of mine — the former roommate of my dear great-aunt — now lives. Operated by the local municipality, it is well-run, clean, bright, cheery, and functional. There are games rooms (where the residents gather for exercises and bridge and piano sing-alongs) and a pleasant staff, and if the rooms are tiny (with just enough room for a bed, a dresser, and a picture or two), the common rooms are large and inviting. It, too, is an overwhelmingly sad place, where old people go when their seventy or eighty or ninety years can fit in a small suitcase.

Most of the people in such institutions, and most of the people in my mother's apartment building are women: In the former, they outnumber the men by a ratio that is even scarier than you find in most home-economics classes. In the latter, most of the residents are like my mother, either widows or nursing frail, elderly husbands — just as my mother nursed my dad for so many months. It makes you wonder not why women live an average of seven years longer than men, but why the hell we would want to.

My mother may not like it (indeed, I am quite sure she won't), but if push ever comes to shove, and she can't stay in her apartment any longer, I will move her in with me. She may fight me tooth and nail, but if I have to I'll keep her locked in a small room at the top of the stairs (like something out of a Bette Davis movie), at least until I can ply her with enough chocolate to change her mind. But I will be damned if someone I love spends the last years of her life being addressed as "Mrs. B." by a bunch of poorly paid strangers in soft-soled white shoes. If she must be bossed around and watched over, it will be by her daughter, even if I call her, on occasion, You Old Bat.

Surviving Superwoman

To be harsh about it, the single-income family is dead in the water. Very few families have the economic wherewithal to live on one salary; very few women have the self-confidence to admit that (a) they would rather stay home with their kids; or (b) they are not necessarily fulfilled by carrying a briefcase, no matter how soft the leather. Even very rich women feel obliged to have a little public-relations consulting business, a small boutique — at the very least, a reason to "do lunch" every day.

We all know that this has all sorts of ramifications for society, and that they are undoubtedly of great importance. I am consoled by the thought that, somewhere, civil servants burn the noon oil in an effort to determine trends and make sociological sense of this stuff. What worries me is that all over the country, poor, confused husbands and children and dogs are learning firsthand that, though work may well make the average female feel complete, it can also make her crabby.

Basically, there are two distinct kinds of working wife-mothers. There are those who never stop working, who drop their children with chilling efficiency and without breaking stride, taking off, at most, the maternity leave allotted to them (and sometimes only the afternoon). And there are those who leave the work force, generally until their children enter school full time. When they go back to work, they are hit with an overwhelming panic that the world has passed them by, and throw themselves headlong into career catchup, which means overtime. Both types are scary and unnerving: Who, their families wonder, is this snarly, drawn person, and how can they ever get her attention again?

In the first scenario, the concerned husband and infant child ought to schedule an appointment with the wife-mother. Since she is generally up at the crack of dawn and home long after both husband and infant are asleep, the only way to do this is to phone her office, arranging for the infant to be making soft, sad, chirpy noises in the background. If the pair can get past the wife-mother's administrative assistant to the wife-mother herself, they should book a formal half-hour "information meeting".

In the second scenario, such a ruse would have no effect at all. Wife-mothers who go back into the work force are usually so harried, they would likely put the husband and child on hold, not recognizing their voices.

However, the family has one advantage: It is likely that when the wife-mother made her decision to return to her career, she insisted upon getting, from the husband and child, a certain amount of cooperation about the home — help with household chores, meal preparation, etc., etc. The best way, then, for the family to get the wife-mother to sit up and take notice is to stop all such efforts, immediately. Beds should be left unmade, dishes undone, meals unplanned; newspapers should be allowed to stack up, vacuuming ignored, garbage not taken out; the cat's litter box should not be touched.

Quite quickly, the wife-mother will call a family meeting to discuss the problem, at which point the husband and child can bring up the real issue — their feeling of abandonment and wish to return to the good old days, when the wife-mother had more time and less edge to her voice.

That, alas, is only a dream, for most women quite rightly enjoy working, and most families need them to do so. But the bottom line is this:

The eighties' codeword for crabbiness is "stress", and women are taking everything for it (special vitamins, calcium, dips in tranquility tanks, massages) except what they should, which is two consecutive days off once in a while. That's all the modern family can ask; it's not too much to expect the modern woman to give.

Everyone might also remember that — until there are Supermen, who clean house, do laundry, make meals, and work full time (not to mention building award-winning furniture in their spare moments), and until there are self-cleaning, self-feeding, and self-changing Superbabies (who occasionally read themselves bedtime stories), and until there are well-adjusted, secure, and acne-free Superteens (who voluntarily clean their rooms) — striving to be Superwoman is an exercise if not in futility, at least in thankless nobility: you end up a martyr.

Invading Hordes

Sooner or later, it's going to happen:

Someone is going to come into your house and live with you and your family. It may be your mother or her step-father, your unemployed sister or his ex-con nephew, your pregnant teenage cousin or her destitute uncle — or someone you pay (a nanny or a nurse) or one who pays you (a tenant or a boarder). It doesn't really matter why it is doomed to happen (though that's easy: nowhere in North America are there enough cheap places for people to live when they find themselves in trouble), or who the offending party is (though somehow, it is likely to be a relative), or that you may, for a moment or two, even feel noble, offering up your castle as shelter. What matters is that you know this will happen, and that your life will never be the same.

A few years ago, my husband and I, then living in a large, decidedly unrenovated building, had a friend of ours move in with us. (His name, incidentally, was Bones. People who move in with people tend to have names like Bones: Gus, Mac, Leroy, Dr. Dance, etc.) Anyway, Bones was (and is) a nice fellow, and when he found himself in a spot of difficulty (an estranged wife and new baby to support and immense debts), he took over the vacant second floor of our building.

There, for what it's worth, he had five rooms to himself, including a bathroom and fully equipped kitchen. He could have gone forever without seeing either of us. As quickly became apparent, however, he did not merely want to live in our house, he wanted to be part of our family. Where once the first thing we heard in the morning was the alarm clock, we began to hear Bones's step on the stairs and his hearty cry of, "Any coffee on?" Little by little, things of his started invading our living quarters. First was the large jar of what appeared to be miniature fetuses that showed up in the fridge. (They turned out to be nude, home-bottled pears.) Then, a half-eaten box of Shreddies, which appeared, one moment, on the kitchen counter; the next, in the cupboard; the next, in the magazine rack in the john. Things of ours also began disappearing: ashtrays, coffee cups, newspapers.

When the shower in his bathroom broke, he began (quite naturally) using ours, and a whole trail of things appeared: a new kind of shampoo, a third razor on the bathtub ledge, an extra towel.

Eventually, people began to show themselves, too: His

infant daughter, complete with toys, walkers, and soothers; his bizarre collection of friends for poker games. Then there were the phone calls from collection agencies, bookies, and fellow gamblers, and so many from his estranged wife that I soon was able to recognize her ring.

Throughout it all, Bones remained what he had always been — a pleasant, not unthoughtful but irresponsible young guy. His stay with us didn't turn his life around, though it may have bought him some breathing space. Certainly he was grateful for the refuge. Several months after he moved in, he moved out again — it was quite easy, as he had never unpacked — without, I suspect, any idea of how he had altered our lives.

There are countless people like Bones around, be they friend or relative. Should you be moved to invite them in out of the cold for a time there are some things to remember:

Do not believe you are prepared. You may imagine that by installing an extra bathroom in the basement or raising the roof in the attic, you have cut off potential problems at the pass. You may even be so naive as to think that because you have done the Right Thing (by opening your door to one in need), you will get your just rewards.

On all counts, you will be wrong.

When a new person moves in, a house immediately shrinks by half its size. This is not unlike what occurs in a household with cats: one cat in a house feels like one cat, and may be a pleasure; two cats feel like four cats, and may be a pain in the ass; a third cat feels like thirteen, and you spend most of your life with your head in the litter box. Same thing when a new person moves in, even a small, short person who could fit in your broom closet. The house is immediately crowded.

Second thing: No matter how separate and isolated you have arranged his living space, he will spend his time in your kitchen, drinking coffee. No one knows why this happens, but it does. You will lose all semblance of privacy: no more pillow fights with your naked spouse; no more baby-talk to the dog; no more scratching your crotch; no more nonchalance when you forget to flush the toilet. From the moment a new person enters your home, you must be on guard. And dressed.

Third thing: Though you may pretend otherwise, you will, somewhere in your heart, have secret plans for the new person. If he's broke, you will hope he takes advantage of your kindness to get out of debt; if he is unemployed, you will hope he finally finds The Job; if he's in trouble with the law, you will hope he goes straight, etc. Such hope springs eternal; it is also fated to die of disappointment — not because people want to disappoint you, but because past the age of eleven or twelve, most of us don't change very much. Thus, the con man will likely stay a con man; the young man who can't keep a job will likely be unable to keep one at fifty; the young whore will grow up to be an old one.

This isn't, I think, a cynical view. Realistically, when you invite a loved one to "move in with us for a few months until you get on your feet again" you're asking for a broken heart, especially if what you really mean is, "We're giving you a chance, so don't screw it up". (By the way, that reminds me: The "few months" can quickly turn into a few years. It isn't only landlords who have difficulty getting folks to move out.)

Don't be discouraged: The world is a lousy place sometimes, and there are lots of folks who need a break. Good for you if you can help give them one. All I ask is that you bear in mind three things: One, you'll never be naked again; two, you'll never be alone again; three, don't expect to be thanked and showered with praise for your kindness. You won't be, and you shouldn't be. Virtue is its own reward. I guess that's why it's a virtue.

The Family as India

We have some friends who run their family as though it were a Third World country with its first elected government. They live in a state of reasonably benign confusion, where nothing — from the dishes to major decisions — gets done without a formal vote or, at least, a show of hands.

The parents are good small-l liberals, who pride themselves on their progressive thinking. They believe as a matter of principle that one does not tell a child what to do, one inquires as to how the child feels about it, then asks if he would like to do it. Since the day they were born, their two daughters (one nine, the other twelve, and both cunning beyond their years) have been consulted about every move the parents have made on their behalf, every extracurricular activity they joined, every vacation the family took. By the time they were nine months old (when they realized that if they did not scream, Mummy and Daddy would never change their sopping diapers), they understood that their parents were incapable of decision-making unless it was quasi-communal and democratic. Of course, they became gifted manipulators.

Here is a sample conversation — or rather, "family forum", as the McBrides like to call it:

Rick, the daddy: "Tara and Michelle, Melinda [that's the mummy; the family is on a first-name basis] and I are toying with the idea of us all going to the Rockies this summer. What do you think?"

Tara, nine: "That sounds okay."

Michelle, twelve: "That sucks."

Rick: "Only 'okay', Tara? Do you think it sounds fun, or would you miss your friends in the city too much? Or would you rather go to Grandma's cottage again?"

Tara: "I don't know."

Michelle: "I'd rather get a job at the Ex this summer."

Melinda: "Now Michelle, we've already discussed that, remember? We agreed that you're really too young to have a job. Remember what Rick said — you'll have lots of time to work once you're sixteen?"

Tara: "I want a job too, Melinda."

Rick: "Honey, I'm afraid you're much too young. Remember how we studied about the laws in Ontario that protect children from being sent out to work? Remember that?"

Michelle: "But I need to buy a ton of things this summer. I need some new tops and a bike and stuff . . ."

Tara: "Me too, and I wanna get *Ponga* for the computer!"

Rick: "Maybe it is time we reviewed their allowances, Mel . . ."

After a vote (unanimous, of course), the family decided to increase the girls' already vast allowances, and they went nowhere that summer — except for Labor Day weekend at Grandma's cottage. During July and August, all votes regarding holidays resulted in a 2-2 deadlock. (Grandma finally cast the tie-breaking vote out of desperation to see Tara and Michelle.)

This was a great pity, for Rick was dying to see the Rockies, and Melinda had deigned to grow a little excited at the prospect. What they should have done, of course, was present the trip plans to the children as fait accompli, which is what smart parents have been doing for years. What they should have done, in other words, was be fascists. Once again, they made the critical error of treating the family unit as a democracy, a noble but flawed concept: Surely no one really believes that small, short, young persons who, when faced with a question they cannot answer, reply, "We haven't taken that yet", are full family partners. One of the best reasons to have children is to guarantee that for at least sixteen years, one will have someone to boss around. Moreover, one will always have a built-in excuse to go to interesting places on the pretext of it Being Good For The Kids.

Parents who forget this deserve what they get — a lot of grief and lousy vacations.

PART TWO: State of the Heart

Cruel and Unusual Punishers

They are legion, or so it sometimes seems — men and women (but mostly men) who are, as eighties-speak would have it, incapable of commitment.

Sprinters all, good only for the short, hard distance, they have neither the heart nor the stomach for marriage or a relationship that requires the same staying power and can bring the same satisfactions. They like the chase, but not the catch; the hunt, but not the kill; the start, but not the finish. At the merest suggestion of dependency or emotional need, they either back off entirely or turn cruel and cold. An adoring look can chill their blood, a whispered "I love you" freeze-dries them: Children in adult bodies, they are so self-absorbed that there is no room in their lives for anyone else.

Probably, there have always been a few of them with us, emotional cripples posing as madcap bachelors; but it is nonsense to pretend that there have always been so many of them, or that they have always had such a choice of willing victims, or that they are anything but dangerous. It is also foolish, in this egalitarian, share-the-blame era, to pretend that there are as many women like them.

There aren't.

Only one woman I know is like them, as cool, as manipulative, as hurtful. Other women I know may be too keen to find a mate, too eager to please, too insecure, whatever — but they are infinitely nicer human beings than the men they meet.

Aaaah yes, the men they meet.

You have read the books and magazine stories with the tricky titles; a recent one that I remember, because every single woman I know read at least parts of it, was called *Women Who Love Too Much.* Its premise is that women who badly want a mate scare prospective ones away by being too demanding. If I had a buck for every woman friend who said to me, when this drivel was everywhere you looked, "Maybe it's me . . .", I would own a château in the south of France. I know the men these women were involved with; it wouldn't have mattered if they'd been as independent and aloof and undemanding as your average house cat, these guys would not have stuck around.

I remember a telephone conversation I heard between one of these friends and one of these men. To appreciate it fully, you should know that they had met, about eighteen months earlier, in a bar.

He was the instigator, the approacher, the mover. He was utterly captivated by her. He loved her looks, he said. He loved her tall, fit body, her laugh. Not surprisingly (what heart wouldn't melt, hearing this from a nice-looking member of the opposite sex?), she thought him rather charming. He walked her home that night; the next day, he phoned: Could he see her soon? He missed her. For the next month, he courted her. He phoned her constantly, each time filling her in on his every move (so she would know where he was, and that he longed for her). He very soon told her how much he loved her a dozen times a day; he held her hand and bragged of how proud he was to be with someone so lovely.

When they slept together, he was a skilled lover and, more important, he loved to touch her. He kept an arm around her always, a hand on her back, and constantly told her how fine and exciting her body was.

After perhaps another month she felt confident enough of him (and Them) to introduce him to her family and her friends. He went to dinner at her mother's; he was silent, almost surly, and impolite. Once, they came out for dinner with David and me; this time, he was aggressive, almost antagonistic. Not once during the evening did he touch her, and whenever she touched him (a hand on his knee, nothing blatant or possessive), he flinched.

One weekend, they had arranged to visit a couple she knew. The time came for him to pick her up; he wasn't there. She waited and waited; but he never arrived, and never phoned. The next day, still expecting him to call, she waited some more. Nearly frantic, she called him. The line was out of service, the operator said, and the new number was unlisted.

He did call — two months later. He was profusely apologetic, crying on the phone. He'd made a terrible mistake; could they meet and talk? She was just beginning to get over the hurt, but she was also curious, so she agreed.

When they met, it was as if they had never been apart. He had some problems, he said. His parents had been uncaring, and it had made him leery of love, but he'd read a self-help book, and recognized himself in it. Now, he said, he was ready. Ready for love, ready for her. He would prove he was also deserving of her. God, how he loved her.

He talked of flying to Paris, to get married. Maybe even children. It lasted, like this, for another two months. Then, he began commenting on her weight (she had been skipping her fitness classes to be with him, but if she'd gained any weight, we couldn't see it). He'd look at her and shake his head. "That isn't the face I fell in love with," he'd say. "That isn't that slim body."

He started to go out nights with friends he had never mentioned before. He was deliberately evasive about where he'd been, even though he was usually only at evening classes or out for a walk. Soon, he was criticizing everything:

Why did she wear that dress? Why did her stupid aunt always say how pretty she looked, when she wasn't? Why did her mother phone so often? Why was she so busy with work — didn't she have any other interests?

Christmas, their first together, came and went. She gave him small, sweet gifts; he gave her a six-pack of his favorite beer. She suggested a walk in the snow, just being together; he announced he was heading home to his parents' place for a few days. She looked forward to Yuletide fêtes; he refused to go anywhere.

How kind and affectionate and wonderful he had been; he was a different man now. On the rare occasions they made love (her body was not sexy any more, he said), he went back to his apartment as soon as the act was complete. He refused to let her touch him, even his hand, when they were in public.

She must have done something wrong, she thought. She began pleading, "Do you love me?"; at best, the answer was, "I don't know." She asked him to tell her, please, whenever she did something irritating; he was happy to oblige.

Sometime after Christmas, she went on a trip with a male cousin, hoping to sort out her feelings for the man. When she returned, he was not at the airport. He was not at home. There was no note. A week later, he called. Where had he been? "Oh," he said, "I've been busy." For the next six weeks they saw each other when he felt like it; he allotted her a night every week or so, and would change plans, often the day before. She considered herself lucky if he let her kiss him. She didn't fall apart, but came close to it. One night, she phoned to ask if she could come over for coffee, and was met with a sharp "No!" and outright hostility. They quarreled.

It was over, she said when I saw her the next morning.

Then the phone rang.

"So what was your problem last night?" His voice was flat, devoid of emotion.

"My problem? I just wanted to see you."

"I don't want to see you."

"But why did you come back in my life? Why did you call

me? Why did you say we might still get married, as long as there'd be no children and I kept my shape? Why did you say that?"

"It was easier," he said, "than telling you what I really felt."

Weeping, she summoned up her last reserves of courage and pride. "I don't think we should go through this again," she said. "I don't think we should see each other again. It's too hard on me . . ."

"Okay," said the man, as chipper as though a golf game had just been cancelled. "That's fine." And he hung up.

By wooing her with kindness and praise, then turning on her, he destroyed her confidence in her looks, in her ability to do her job, in herself. Whenever he sensed her close to breaking things off, he would love her and thrill her by being merely courteous. The second she was back on the hook, he would abandon her. Up and down, in and out, he played her like a fish you catch, only to throw it back, and catch it again.

He was no weird, one-in-a-million psychotic. She has seen men like him before — we have seen this happen, again and again, to our splendid female friends. He is just one of a common type.

From my safe distance, I have noticed a couple of things. Most of these men are reasonably attractive and articulate. They also seem to be from a social class below the women they pursue and then hurt. If that sounds vaguely British and archaic, well, so be it. North America, too, is still divided into social classes. All these men could easily make the leap upwards by virtue of their brightness and charm and ambition; and it seems that it is the very "class" that they initially like so much in the women they chase. Yet they appear incapable of actually bridging the small gap. It's as though they want to woo these highfalutin women — independent, and well-spoken professionals — to prove they can "get" them. Then, they turn resentful and degrade them.

That's my dime-store analysis of it, anyway. I'm not really interested in what makes them tick, though I wonder if there is a single, widely applicable societal explanation for them. I don't care if they had terrible childhoods, bad first love affairs, or are mentally ill. What I care about is that, as my husband often says, the world's full of great women and really lousy men.

And what I wish, more than anything, is that the bastards would leave my friends alone.

Condom Sense

People learn everything faster when they are young, and fearless, and stupid, and in the grip of raging hormones: This is equally true of downhill skiing, roller-skating, gymnastics, and buying and using condoms. For other generations, condoms were a part of their growing up. They had all manner of nicknames for them (French safes, rubbers, etc.) and expressions about them ("like having a bath with your clothes on"). But my generation has no condom sense at all, which is also why we are the only people other than the clergy to call them by their rightful name. As young women, most of us were on the birth-control pill, which was both easy to get (in that you obtained it, like antibiotics, on a doctor's prescription) and easy on the conscience (you could pretend you needed it for your acne or erratic periods). As young men, most of us didn't give birth control a second thought. Now, as adults, we find ourselves in the age, not of Aquarius, but of AIDS, herpes, and other sexually transmitted diseases. For the first time in our lives, we have to come to terms with buying condoms, not to mention using them and trying to render them sexy. It is not a simple task. Some guidelines:

Buying them

1. Enter drugstore where you have never been before.
2. Grab shopping cart.

3. Tour store, throwing into cart at least four items from each aisle. Sample-sized bottles of shampoo, creme rinse, after-shave, etc. are especially good; they fill the cart and won't break the bank.

4. With cart at least half-full, stop at condom section. Treat this section as you would any other, that is, do not be afraid to comparison-shop, look for specials, and check brands. Force yourself to appear confident and unembarrassed; choose the kind you want. Buy in bulk so you never have to repeat this procedure.

5. Lurk near cashier until (a) there is no lineup because (b) the store is empty. Be prepared to lurk awhile, unless you can shop during off-hours, say, after midnight.

6. Begin unloading stuff. UNLOAD CONDOMS FIRST. This will insure they are the first items put in the bag. Engage cashier in interesting, diverting conversation, such as a discussion of free trade. DO NOT GET FLUSTERED AND SAY "FREE LOVE" BY MISTAKE.

7. Exit store. Wipe off forehead sweat. Go home.

(Many of these hints have been adapted from the advice found in *The Teenage Girl's Guide to Buying Tampons for the First Time.* Reprinted with thanks.)

Using them

1. The woman should regard the condom as she would an expensive pair of nylons or panty hose, and not as a sock. This will help her, if only by accident, to handle the male organ with a certain gentleness, and not as a football.

2. The man should remember that the condom is not something to be avoided until the very last possible second, when he may be otherwise preoccupied and his hand-organ coordination less than optimal. The condom is not an orgasm-enhancer, it is a disease- and baby-preventing agent and, to be effective, must not be treated as an afterthought.

Making them sexy

This is not impossible, but it is tricky. It is easier to remember the Don'ts:

1. No matter how many ads your local health department/

safe-sex committee/prostitutes'-rights group publishes to the contrary, do not practice your condom skills on a banana. While it may make you better at putting on a condom, it is also likely to make you break into hysterical laughter (or worse, bizarre monkey imitations) at the crucial moment, which is rude and withering.

2. Avoid gimmicky condoms — flavored or scented ones in particular. Strawberry-flavored lipstick didn't sell either. Only pedophiles wish to pretend they are with a twelve-year-old during sex; only morons want to smell of bubble gum after it.

NOTE: In recent months, certain health professionals have been advising sexually active persons to use rubber "dental dams" (the kind used by dentists performing root canals) during oral sex. It is my opinion that if we have come to the point where there is any link between oral sex and oral surgery, we should forget it, and take up euchre.

When Divorce Is Out of the Question

Tammy Wynette hasn't done a hurtin' song about it yet, but if she did, it would be called "M-U-R-D-E-R". I can hear it now:

Oh, spare your wife from stares of pity,
You don't have to treat her shitty;
Save her heart and save her head,
What you do is kill her dead,
Oh what you do is kill her dead.

So maybe it's not the country classic "D-I-V-O-R-C-E": Rich folks have never gone much for country anyway. But they sure have come up with an interesting alternative to marriage breakup. God forbid they should bring shame upon their unwanted spouses (think what people would say!).

What they do instead is (a) blow them or (b) have them blown away.

A few years back several prominent-type Canadians (one the son of a prairie premier, another an ostensibly devout self-made Ontario millionaire, were charged and convicted in the deaths of their wives. Well, said the self-made millionaire, his poor wife was against divorce (and, heck, so was he for that matter). In order to spare her the humiliation of a public breakup, he did the decent thing and hired someone to kill her.

The idea seems to have caught on: Just a couple of years ago, another well-known Canadian businessman was unable to accept the fact that his wife was in love with someone else. He went to jolly old England and shot the poor fellow dead. The businessman testified that he'd tried everything to keep the marriage together: he'd even brought his wife flowers and bought her gifts. Still, she would have nothing to do with him. I can almost see him helplessly shrugging his shoulders, as if to ask, "What other option did I have?"

Obviously, it is time for an impartial observer to weigh the various merits of divorce and murder:

Cost

It is doubtful that a contracted-out murder is more expensive than any divorce other than the simple, uncontested sort. But then, if you are able to shake hands and part, there would be no need to consider murder, so we shall rule that one out. In fact, a long, drawn-out divorce (complete with a custody battle and prenuptial contract to argue over, through lawyers) is likely to cost you more in the end. And, obviously, there is no comparison if you perform the murder yourself; in this case, the only expenses are the tools required for the job.

Speed

This is easy. A murder is much less time-consuming than even the quickest divorce. One might say that murder is to divorce what dictatorship is to democracy. The former is infinitely more efficient.

Neatness
Apart from the immediate physical unpleasantness of murder, a divorce is, in terms of emotional and fiscal aftermath, far messier. An ex-spouse is likely to haunt your life — phoning, turning up at your favorite restaurants, demanding higher support payments, sending threatening letters, etc., etc. A dead spouse, once out of your life, stays out forever.
Repercussions
With murder, there is either one huge repercussion (you get caught and go to jail) or none; with divorce, however, your family may be annoyed; your friends may ally themselves with your former mate (thereby requiring you to make new pals, which is a bother); the emotional duress may cause you to become distracted or inefficient at the office. Worst of all, divorce leads to uncontrollable gossip.

Murder leads to death. Period.

It's no contest, really, is it? And no darn wonder the rich get richer and the poor get poorer: The stupid poor keep getting divorced and splitting their assets.

A Tale of Two Cities

Twenty years ago, the truly chic had an "open marriage": you-do-your-thing and I'll-do-mine and when-we're-together-it-will-be-because-we-REALLY-want-to-be-together. These days, that couple on the cutting edge is involved in a long-distance relationship: you-do-your-thing-in-Boston and I'll-do-mine-in-Montreal and when-we're-together-it-will-be-because-we-met-by-accident-at-an-airport.

The benefits of long-distance relationships are said to be many: neither member of the couple is smothered; both are free to pursue a career and keep his/her independence. Without the day-to-day grind of running a house and the forced intimacy of bathroom and breakfast table, time together remains special and fresh. Because such moments *à deux* are rare, they are more romantic.

What they don't tell you, of course, is that you are also likely to end up with a relationship less intimate than the one my mother has with her hairdresser: They see each other only every eight weeks or so, their time together is certainly special. They are always uncommonly civil to one another; this is surely right for a woman who wants neat, well-cared-for hair but of questionable value for someone who wants anything more.

Familiarity, in other words, may very well breed contempt, not to mention quarrels over the dishes. He can tell, from your charming mood changes, that your period is twelve minutes away; and you know when his hemorrhoids are back with a vengeance. But the other thing it breeds is, well, familiarity. In the long run, that not only keeps people together, it makes them want to stay that way.

I know several couples who went the long-distance-love route, right down to maintaining separate residences in separate cities (in one case, on separate continents), separate sets of friends, separate cars, separate bank accounts, and a policy of one giving the other formal notice when he/she was coming to town. They would go weeks and sometimes months without seeing each other and, in the beginning, their infrequent meetings were certainly more highly charged than any scenes from a traditional marriage: They'd meet for dinner in a posh restaurant, and, barely able to keep their hands off each other long enough to finish the espresso, would taxi home to fall into bed for a night of abandon.

As time went by, alas, they had less and less to say to each other over the swell dinners; the taxi rides were permeated by uncomfortable silences; and the sex, though still newish and therefore exhilarating, left both parties feeling rather empty in the morning. In every case, the marriages collapsed quickly (one lasted six months, the others less than two years), and the parties even had trouble summoning up enough passion to make the divorces bitter and interesting.

It strikes me that one of the reasons people bother getting married is because they want to go beyond the self-conscious politesse and small courtesies of perpetual dating, which, though pleasant, do not allow one the freedom to pick one's nose or blow a wicked raspberry in bed. This may seem an odd way to judge one of our most treasured institutions, but I believe that human beings are not meant to always be on their best behavior, always coiffed and groomed to the nines, always making witty conversation. All of us have a need to be mundane or trite sometimes, to schlepp about the house in a disgusting sweatsuit, to eat Kraft Dinner and admit that we like it. We also have a need do all this with someone.

Marriage is about love, sure; but it's also about trusting the other guy so much you know he will love you even if he catches you tenderly squeezing your pimples in the loo. In short, it's about sharing, the one thing that is truly and totally precluded by the long-distance relationship. Unless you share a house and a life and the whole dreary business of living together, it's awfully difficult to harvest the other stuff — the in-jokes, the intimacy of understanding that he wants to leave that party *now* (all from the way he lifted an eyebrow), the thrill of knowing someone almost as well as you do yourself.

My parents, like so many other young couples caught up in the Second World War, were separated for years. When my dad finally returned home after the war, my brother, then a little boy, didn't recognize him, and ran away crying from this tall stranger who wanted to hug him. This went on for several weeks, I'm told, and it almost broke my father's heart. But he persevered, of course, and the little boy grew used to him, came to him for goodnight kisses, and all was well.

My mother has never said so, but I'm sure she felt a little of that strangeness, too, though if it happened, they were able to work it out. My dad, like the other young men of his generation, had little choice: his country was at war, and he was a part of it. How awful it must be to be the eighties version of my mother or my father — to greet an unfamiliar spouse at an airport, and to know that he/she is unfamiliar only because you both wanted it that way, that you have no war to blame.

During the sixties, I wondered why people wanted "open marriages"; I always thought the only marriage worth having is the one that is closed. Ditto for the long-distance relationship: It's one of those contradictory phrases, like "military intelligence". It doesn't make any sense. The only tale of two cities that works is Dickens's; when fiction becomes fact, it's likely to be only the worst of times, not the best.

Buyer Beware

A friend of mine met his wife through a personal ad in a Montreal newspaper.

I haven't a clue how she described herself or what he said in his reply; but, somehow, they found each other, went on a blind date to a Hallowe'en party (for which she dressed in so many layers of clothes that it wasn't until their second date that he discovered she was a slim, long-legged creature and not, as he'd thought, an engaging giantess), and ended up married. That was almost fifteen years ago.

Personal ads (then often placed, as a joke, by groups of women who'd had too much wine and, giggling and filled with false courage, phoned their local papers to advertise for brunch partners) are still around, which is still a little embarrassing to most of us. What kind of world do we live in, we wonder, when in order to meet someone, you have to advertise? Isn't it a sad commentary on our society that Companions Wanted sections exist?

Hell, no. Who doesn't want a companion — and why should you be the object of patronizing pity if you admit to it and find one through a newspaper advertisement? Is meeting someone this way any sadder than meeting someone the way people used to, twenty-five years ago, when they gathered to dance in basements of churches they never attended and didn't believe in? I think not.

The only real problem with Companions Wanted ads is the one you find with advertising in general — that is, sifting through the hard-sell gloss to determine the merits of the product. Truth has never been an essential ingredient in advertising. One knows that, despite the NO MONEY DOWN, NO INTEREST EVER, NO PAYMENTS UNTIL 1992 claims of the discount furniture outlets, one is going to have to pay something, sometime. One should also know that the "attractive young redhead" who "loves long walks on exotic beaches and moonlight cruises" is probably looking for a sugar daddy. In both one must separate the wheat from the chaff.

Some phrases and catchwords are dead giveaways:

First, the key abbreviations. SWM has nothing to do with a fondness for swimming or other aquatic sports; it means Single White Male. SWF is Single White Female; GWM is Gay White Male; GBF is Gay Black Female, etc., etc.

The words "adventurous" or "experimental", when used to describe a couple, do not mean the pair is keen on mountain-climbing, trekking, or hang-gliding. "Discreet" always means that respondees must be prepared to sneak around because the advertiser is either gay but not out of the closet or married and content to stay that way.

Most persons advertising for "v gdlkg" (very good-looking) others tend not to be interested in serious, long-term relationships.

"Eclectic" does not mean the advertiser has a wide range of interests. It really means she does not like *Hockey Night in Canada*.

Mature self-employed businessmen advertising for female companions do not want replies from equally mature businesswomen. This is why their ads establish age limits, usually right up front. They begin with the age of consent and never go much higher, that is, "If you are between 18 and 25". Age limits are the *only* thing you can always believe, and take at face value, in a personal ad. If the ad attempts to restrict replies to those under thirty, and you are thirty-five, do not bother answering it. A young woman I know once answered a "mature businessman" ad, which prescribed an upper age limit of thirty-five. She was stunned to receive a phone call from a well-known Toronto furrier, then fifty-two. "Why did you ask for replies from women twenty-five to thirty-five?" she asked. "Oh," said the man, ingenuously, "I don't get along with women in my age bracket."

People who describe themselves as sincere in their ads usually are; those who say they are fit (and demand replies from fit others) often aren't. The fitness requirement in a Companions Wanted ad frequently means "big tits".

In short, Companions Wanted ads are just another tracking device for the search for a kindred spirit, and there is nothing shameful or desperate about it. Remember, however, that, as with all other advertised goods and services, the rule of thumb with these ads is simple: *Caveat emptor.*

First Kiss, Revisited

They were on the couch, nuzzling.

"Ohhhh, Leo," said my friend in a throaty moan of pleasure. The second the words were out of her mouth, she almost passed out in horror: Leo was a man with whom she'd lived for years and from whom she'd been separated only a few months. The man on the couch with her, alas, was not Leo, but Gordon, and he was not impressed. In fact, so unimpressed was he that he stomped out of her living room, her house, and her life.

He was, at the time, thirty-three; she was thirty-six, an attractive single woman with a good job, her own house, nice clothes, and a great deal to offer. What, I wonder, was old Gordon's problem? Did he imagine he was her first and only lover? Had she lived all those years without at least the occasional man in her life? She had not, as it happened, been thinking of Leo at that critical moment (although if she had, it would have been understandable, if not wholly forgivable). The name, from years of habit, had simply come unbidden to her lips. The last time she had been with a man, on a couch, in a wonderfully compromising position, the man had been Leo.

The whole foolish incident, though embarrassing, should have caused only a ripple of discomfort. Instead, it sent Gordon running. It is a lovely illustration of the difficulty that many of us have with Adult Dating.

I do wish there were a better word: Dating is what we did in high school, and is so evocative of parental inspections and sweaty armpits and coy sexual behavior that it's no wonder some of us, like Gordon — surprised to find ourselves still doing it so long after graduation — handle the tricky parts with all the maturity of a teenage boy who discovers his steady necking with someone else.

How do fully grown adults who have been through the relationship mill a time or two handle the First Kiss, when they've had dozens of First Kisses, some of which led not only to dancing, but wedlock? As one man, about to be single again, confessed to me, "I don't know if I'm ready to go through all that stuff again — walking someone to her front door, figuring out if I should ask myself in. I'm thirty-nine years old, for Christ's sake."

How do you proceed in a new relationship when you bring to it an ex-spouse, a lover or two, perhaps a child here and there? It would be ludicrous to play the perpetual virgin (if not physically, then emotionally); my single friends always complain that things happen too fast in Adult Dating: You tell each other too much too soon; you sleep together too soon; you "go steady" too soon; you move in together too soon; and worst of all, often it's over too bloody soon.

Difficulties aside, for those of us unwilling or unable to afford marriage again, who can't find the right person to persuade them otherwise, who are widowed, divorced, or single by choice, dating is not the road to a real relationship, but a permanent state. And when compared to the alternative, which is no dating and no contact with the opposite sex (let alone sex with the opposite sex), dating is infinitely preferable.

Despite how you feel, say, at the end of a first date, which is curiously like how one felt at the end of a first date at sixteen, you are not a teenager anymore, and need not act like one.

Teenagers may feel they have to kiss/neck/sleep together early on in a relationship; adults can say no, thank you, to any of the above without feeling an obligation to do otherwise. The delightful corollary, of course, is that adults can also say yes, please, to any of the above without worrying what their friends might think. Teenagers may also feel obliged to marry everyone with whom they sleep; adults feel obliged only to be civil to them, and treat them kindly. Teenagers find silence uncomfortable, and may fill them by spilling their guts about their innermost secrets, thoughts, and desires; adults know they should do this only after the silences have grown comfortable.

And, oh yes, although teenagers may take offence at being addressed by the wrong name at a tender moment, adults know this may be merely a function of being an adult who has been involved and in love before — and is capable of doing it all again.

Leave It to Beaver

I was born in the fifties, so I was far too young to have to endure them. Increasingly, however, I feel as though I am getting a second shot at it.

I am not referring to the fifties-nostalgia craze, which has graying forty-five-year-olds who remember the decade with fondness and teenagers stupid enough to deem it romantic — donning poodle skirts and bobby-sox and dancing to "Rock Around the Clock". There is no accounting for taste, and like any fad this will pass, please God.

What is far more worrisome is the other stuff, a climate of fifties morality. "Make room for the Holy Ghost" was the chorus of a thousand Roman Catholic nuns on guard duty at high-school dances, way back then. Well, now too the Holy Ghost and teenage pregnancies comfortably exist side by side, and any given summer is booked, from June through September, with elaborate do-or-die weddings between young people who may have slept together (a furtive poke on the parental couch is more like it) but have certainly never done anything really intimate.

I know several young people, some of them still in their teens, who have in short order: Become engaged (usually on a three- to five-year plan); picked out a lot and snapped up a giant house in the sterile suburbs (complete with family room and fireplace), for which they have also taken out a giant mortgage; signed up for marriage-counseling classes; and then, in a burst of white lace and pale blue tuxedo, walked down the aisle.

I know several other young people, some of them still in their teens, who have in short order: Become or got a girlfriend pregnant; abandoned plans for college or travel and settled into a life of poverty, lousy jobs, and subsidized daycare. Choice, the great rallying cry of my generation, goes unexercised by many modern teenagers. Few of the young people I know live together before marriage (let alone, live with one or two different lovers); fewer travel to any extent (except the affluent types who go on school-organized tours); and rare among them is the kid with burning ambition.

It is not all as grim as it sounds (some of them will undoubtedly be happy and fulfilled, with lovely children) or perhaps it is grim only to the likes of my twisted mind, but it does contrast strangely with the sixties and seventies when, for most young women, marriage and babies were not the first priority, and when most young men were more interested in backpacking around Europe than in becoming fathers at twenty-one.

I can understand why the teenagers of the fifties were the way they were: Sex education and birth control consisted, respectively, of painful, brief discussions in "Health" class and illegal condoms. The only acceptable relationship was a church- and state-blessed one; there really weren't a whole lot of alternatives. Now, with reasonably graphic sex education in at least some schools (not to mention, horrific AIDS-warning posters that should scare the pants *on* just about anyone), with birth control legal and easier to get (and also abortions, if said birth-control method fails), I am darned if I know why so many youths, as the cops call them, are in such a tear to get married. And the way they're doing it!

Take the white dress: In the fifties, everyone got married in one, it being a symbol of innocence and virginity in which the entire guest list feigned belief — even if the bride was seven months pregnant. And, though you can count on one finger the number of virgins among modern brides, they're wearing white, too — and at as much as $2,000 a pop. Like their counterparts in 1952, they're lining up at china stores to register their dishes.

Most of my friends and I still don't have two plates that match (unless they have the same hotel name on the back), and couldn't give a hoot, but we regularly find ourselves picking out place settings or soup bowls in patterns with dreary names such as Strawberry Fields or Blanc Sur Blanc. Where do young women learn this stuff? I know some of their mothers and I'd bet my bottom dollar they didn't teach them. Why are all the young men so serious, and so eager to burden themselves with wife and family and fieldstone fireplace when they should be spending their money on fast cars and sin?

About a year ago, I was forced to make a trip to an affluent Toronto suburb where some of my young friends live and where others aspire to move. I went there, incidentally, only to see my husband play hockey. (Obviously, I will go anywhere to see a hockey game.)

The houses in the area were all new, all expensive, and indistinguishable, except that house A had, say, a brass street number, and house B had a new bush on the front lawn, and house C was on a prized corner lot (the corner having been artificially created by the builder to fetch a higher price). Most of the homes, three- and four-bedroom jobs, were occupied by bright young couples and their bright young children. Many of the women, I was told by our friends who live there, were full-time housewives and mothers. Most of the men worked in the city, a good hour away.

My husband's game was at the sparkling new athletic complex smack in the middle of the suburb, a monument to the former village's rapidly expanding tax base. The hockey rink is modern and heated; there is a free-form shaped pool, complete with Tarzan rope for swinging, and a giant gymnasium with movable walls for making party rooms and a fitness wing. The several snack bars served not only popcorn and junk food, but also a wholesome array of muffins, juices, yogurts, and trail mix. Trophy cases displayed softball/hockey/swimming ribbons and plaques; bulletin boards were crammed with notices of classes and courses and services.

And yet what should have been the hub of the 'burb had all the warmth of a morgue. Early on a Saturday night, the tropical-plant-filled corridors were all but empty. In the partitioned-off gym, a half-dozen couples, dressed to the teeth, moved morosely on a dance floor while another half-dozen sat, equally grim, at candle-lit tables. The few teenagers appeared bored and unhappy; the handful of parents, youngsters in tow, were cross and didn't exchange even the usual pleasantries between people with kids. Our friends from the area said the complex was always like that, always empty, never alive.

It was all quite curious.

You have to think that part of what drew these young families north to the fields-turned-suburb (in addition, of course, to the fact that they got more house for their buck than in the city) was a search for the homogenous warmth and closeness of the smaller, safer town, a place where the Family was strong and respected, where children could grow up loved and happy — all those things that heat up the television set, and the lonely heart, when old "Leave It to Beaver" reruns are on.

Yet something is missing, just as there is at the "fifties nights" that are everywhere now. The trappings, in both cases, are right — the saddleshoes and ponytails at the dances, the safe neat homes and carefully tended gardens in the suburbs — but the feel is artificial. The men and women who, from a distance, may look like sweet young things, have wrinkles under the eyes and gray in their hair. The bright new communities that look like they're right out of 1955 have little sense of community, perhaps because people don't live there, they sleep there — and still work in the city, downtown, or go to schools miles away.

Perhaps we can go home again, but going back in time is trickier: What we should do, I think, with the fifties is leave it to Beaver.

The Selling of the Househusband

Much has been made of the househusband, that supremely modern fellow who stays at home or works out of it so he may better bond with his children, dust and vacuum the place to within an inch of its life, and shop, cook for, and greet his executive wife when she finally rolls in the door at half-past seven. For a while there, you could not pass a magazine rack without seeing at least one man in an apron, shiny toddlers at his knee, peering out blissfully at you.

It was so touching, so impossibly cool, so too-good-to-be-true that almost no one noticed that (a) it was always the *same* man and (b) that it *was* too good to be true. The househusband, alas, is a mythical creature devised as a stress-reducing device by increasingly desperate working women. Like the little engine that could (I think I can, I think I can), the women quite properly decided that it was all mind over matter. If they could convince themselves that their spouses were doing more at home, being better with the kids, hanging up their clothes, etc., etc., it would *feel* as though they were doing more.

The women began talking it up ("Oh Lenore, my Jerry is getting so much better around the house, he really is . . .") and their magazine-editor-friends picked up on it. Being, by and large, single women, who didn't know any better and believed it to be true, they assigned large numbers of female freelance writers to get the story. All freelance magazine writers are both starving and eager to please; they also know that if an editor says a story is there, it is fucking-well there, and they'd better find it.

The editors of the magazines volunteered their "contacts", the very women who had thought up the idea in the first place. Why yes, their men were doing ever so much more, and yes, some of them had quit their jobs as stockbrokers and opened up "consulting" businesses at home, so they could Be There for the children, etc., etc. (They were hardly going to say that the old man got canned after the crash, now were they?)

Well, the freelance writers heard this, and aside from becoming severely depressed (Why can't we find men like this?), they recognized a great story when they saw it. The editors, of course, were pleased as punch to have their suspicions and foresight and wisdom confirmed as truth, and decided to go with a cover story.

This meant they had to have pictures of a househusband or

two, and a fleet of $400-a-day portrait photographers to do the job.

Well, while alleged househusbands had been happy as clams to lie to the freelance female writers (who are, it should be mentioned, a young and not unattractive lot) and spend hours at chic bars telling them how they found something "comforting" about tucking in the kids at night and a strange sort of fulfilment in cleaning the oven, they were *damned* if they were going to pose for a magazine cover — let alone wearing an apron.

The photographers (all male, and, after days of trying to get the househusbands out of the closet, also pissed off) explained to the female editors that the househusbands refused to cooperate and that, in their opinion, there was no story there.

These are fighting words to female editors, who are always alert to male chauvinists, misogynists, and other manifestations of the White Male Conspiracy. The photographers, they decided, were simply trying to stifle the facts in the hopes that the "threatening" househusband trend would die. In a dozen plant-filled offices the editors were determined to proceed. (This phenomenon is known by editors as Publish And Be Damned and by freelance writers as Fuck The Truth.)

They reassigned the cover photography to the few females working in the business and agreed it would be more prudent, and more fair to the househusbands (who, after all, were risking the scorn of their peers), to use professional models.

Models have their pride, too, however; and all but one refused the assignment on the grounds that posing in an apron would reinforce the widely held stereotype that all male models are gay.

So it came to pass that one male model had his picture taken, in apron, etc., for a plethora of women's magazines; thus were the magazine editors made happy to know they were pushing the edge of the societal envelope; thus did a handful of female freelance writers pay the rent and a few female freelance photographers get some work. Thus was created the mythical househusband.

As for their wives, who started the process by making the whole thing up, well, they're still getting home at half-past seven. And when they walk through that door, they're still finding the men snoozing on the couch, the dishes undone, the beds unmade, and the children — unwashed and unsupervised — in the basement, making caustic-lime pies.

And you know what? T'was ever thus.

On Being Scared Straight

Monogamy is "hot" again. It may not be practiced any more than it ever was, but people are certainly talking about it more. Those once not averse to the occasional affair may be rushing home to dinner with their mates with more regularity; bored housewives may be more reluctant to dally with the delivery boy; middle-aged folks may be enduring mid-life crises without the invigorating benefits of new nookie. Who knows? Who can *ever* know this stuff? Polls and surveys certainly offer no clues; people who answer such surveys lie through their teeth. (Well, I certainly do.)

Like all choices the average human being is required to make in this world, there are good reasons and bad for deciding to be faithful to one's mate.

AIDS is not one of the good ones. We all know the acronym that stands for Acquired Immune Deficiency Syndrome so well that even the *Toronto Star* (a newspaper that would preface a reference to Jesus Christ by reminding its readers that he was "a slim, bearded and devout Nazarene with a close-knit circle of friends") no longer explains it. I have heard countless wives say, in that let's-pretend-I'm-joking voice, when their mate came home late the night before, "Well, at least I know he wasn't out fooling around with a bimbo. That's the one good thing about AIDS." There really is a segment of the population that earnestly hopes that AIDS will scare their spouses into the safety of the marital bed.

Yet the awful disease — that has devastated gay communities throughout North America, moved fearlessly through the ranks of drug addicts, doomed hundreds of babies, and been a living nightmare for hemophiliacs who received transfusions before donor blood was screened for the virus — which now threatens an increasingly nervous and paranoid heterosexual population is no panacea-in-fearsome-disguise for the troubled marriage or wayward spouse. We know that smoking causes lung cancer; a third of Canadians still smoke. That we also know that AIDS is a fatal disease whose primary method of transmission is sexual intercourse is unlikely to scare many of us into being celibate, monogamous, or dedicated (and I mean that in the single-function computer sense) masturbators. In fact, given that we also know the most AIDS-risky sort of sex is of the anal variety, the odds are that we will simply turn into missionary-position evangelists. As horrendous as the threat of AIDS is, I think it unlikely to keep wandering men and women in their own beds. And neither, in my opinion, should it: People who smugly regard AIDS as a guarantee that their spouses will remain faithful to them are the same people who would deliberately get pregnant in order to cement a marriage.

Parenthood and monogamy are not states into which one can be clubbed, no matter how spiked and dangerous the weapon or how gruesome the consequences. All of us can be scared shitless, but it seems worth remembering that if human beings could be scared straight — in any sense — homosexuals would have never left the closet for the bathhouse (a fixture of the gay community that has all but disappeared in the wake of AIDS), and a great many young men would not have died so tragically.

Late Babies, Late Parents

The middle-aged first-time mother, the even-older new father are no longer the oddities you used to read and giggle about in those supermarket tabloids ("New Guinea man fathers child at 90!" "Grandmother of 12 has bouncing baby boy — of her own!"). Many women in their thirties and forties spent the traditional childbearing years in the boardroom; others, married and divorced young, are marrying again and finding there is urgent truth in the cliché about the biological timeclock. Men who have children from a first marriage find themselves acquiescing to their new-child-bride's longing for a baby. There are other men in whom turning forty (or forty-five or fifty) manifests itself in a desire for immortality — which is to say, a child to carry on their name.

Couple all this with the number of men and women who simply decide, rather late in life, that they would love to have kids, and you have, in middle-class North America, a generation of parents, in age and experience rather closer to the rocking chair than to the high chair.

I know a man, about forty-five, who has two children: one a twenty-five-year-old from his first marriage, the other a fifteen-month-old from his second. I know several women who had babies at forty, many who had their first child long past thirty-five. I know a man who became a grandfather the day after he became, again, a father. I know a man whose daughter from his first marriage baby-sits his two daughters from his third. I know a man who fathered one child at twenty-five, got himself a vasectomy at forty, and, at the age of fifty, was back in the same hospital, his testicles the size of footballs and the color of dying bananas, after a vasectomy reversal. (The procedure was successful, incidentally, and a year later he was back at the hospital again to visit his grateful young wife and new baby.)

So what, you ask? Well, both aging new parents and bystanders need help through these tricky times. The etiquette for dealing with a nubile young mother and her taut-bellied young husband simply does not apply to the forty-three-year-old mom and the grinning bald geezer wearing the sweatshirt with "COACH" emblazoned on the sleeve.

Some hints

Mothers-to-be of "a certain age" look foolish in maternity T-shirts with "Baby Under Construction" on the front and a directional arrow pointing to the belly. Actually, all pregnant women look foolish in these shirts, but only aged ones have the wit to *feel* embarrassed in them. Do not force such unseemly gifts upon them, or urge them to buy same.

Never assume, on the basis of a woman's age, that she is merely holding the baby for the real mother. In other words, never approach a woman with babe in arms and say, "Ohhhh, she's beautiful. Whose is she? Looks just like her Grandma!" Always behave as if the woman with the baby is the mother of the baby, even if it strains all credulity.

It is perfectly all right to remark upon the resemblance between a new baby and its aged new father. It is not acceptable to point out that they both have no hair, oddly unfocused eyes, and slightly wizened features.

It is bad form to regale *any* pregnant woman with Horrible Birth Tales — thirty-four-hour labors, breach deliveries, and Babies Born Without Brains. It is particularly cruel to the aged pregnant woman, who is already frighteningly aware that the chances of trouble increase with age.

Do not attempt to comfort the new aged mother by telling her she will get her figure back before she knows it; she may have lost it long ago and would not know it if it hit her in the face.

Gentle folk will never point out, to the aged new parent, that he or she will be collecting baby bonus and old-age pension simultaneously. Neither will they offer themselves up as godparents "just in case something happens". The point is, something already happened: thus, the new baby.

Anyone who volunteers for a lifetime (even a shortened one) of responsibility for another human being deserves the chance to enjoy it.

The Relationship as Corporate Takeover

In keeping with these career-driven times, an increasing number of people approach holy wedlock (and even the unholy sort) with the hard-nosed acumen they bring to business. The process then becomes at least as much fun as the typical wait in one of those frantic, green-walled government offices where herds of people needing passports or driver's licenses line up and fight for the attention of the two surly clerks in the place.

In some circles, prenuptial agreements (specifying who won't get what) are de rigueur, marriage contracts (specifying who won't do what) the rule of thumb. Live-in lovers are routinely given the boot before the standard 50-50 split of assets kicks in; money and property are transferred to untraceable numbered companies before the wedding. I am not talking of the Joan Collinses of this world, but of the Joan Smiths — reasonably average people, albeit often with unreasonably large incomes or the ambition to acquire (and keep) same.

Some say that, in light of spiraling divorce rates, those who view marriage, common-law or otherwise, as a business proposition are smarter than the rest of us. I think that they're a breed apart, all right, but what makes them different is not their cleverness, but their greed.

The relationships I know of that have been set up this way have not been terribly successful. There! the Joan Smiths would say, we told you so: we have to protect ourselves because marriage *is* a measurable risk. Au contraire, from where I sit. It strikes me that when people marry, if there is not some trust, optimism, and a shared, if tentative, assumption that the thing will last, it probably won't. Businesslike relationships will fail, at least in part because they are worked out first on a calculator or in a lawyer's office.

The other reason I think they fail is a sad one. In my limited, vicarious experience, usually only one of the partners wants the contracts and agreements and legalese; the other, eager to please, goes along with it, never dreaming push will come to shove. This was certainly true of one couple of my acquaintance: She was a successful, fast-tracking, and high-priced consultant with a Master of Business Administration degree from a prestigious school and a small family fortune. He was an impoverished, slightly alcoholic, and chronically out-of-work poet. She insisted on the gamut of legal protections: the pre-wedding agreement, the down-to-the-last-detail marriage contract (even to the weekly allowance she would hand over), the safeguarding of certain assets. He feigned nonchalance (hell, maybe he *was* nonchalant) and signed everything she put in front of him, in triplicate.

When the marriage ended, with a whimper rather than a bang, eighteen months later, it was at his instigation. No matter what other problems they had, I am convinced that he had been hurt by her cold, crisp approach to their love, and later insulted by the checks she indifferently sent his way every week. When they parted, he still penniless, she with house and car and bank accounts intact, it was obvious that she was the shattered, unhappy one.

It reminded me, just a little, of the time I was assigned to write about one of those married-swingers' clubs that were briefly popular in the free-and-easy seventies. With a photographer posing as my husband, I went to a dinner-dance held on a boat permanently docked at the Toronto waterfront. It was one of the most ineffably sad evenings I have ever spent.

We met a half-dozen regular couples, and exchanged

phony phone numbers with the duos who took a fancy to us, and wanted to have us "over for dinner". In every case, one partner was obviously hot to trot; the other had been dragged there, unwilling, shamefaced. Perhaps they were told this would make the marriage better, more exciting. God knows what they were told. Sometimes, it was the husband whose eyes would fill up as he saw his spouse on the dance floor, grinding pelvises with a stranger; sometimes, it was the wife. It was horrible to see and I am grateful it was beyond me to imagine what their more intimate encounters might be like, when these poor sad people would be face to face with the awful compromises they had made.

That's what gets me, too, when love is treated with all the warmth of a corporate takeover. It would be bearable, perhaps, if both parties were cool and smart and modern and all for it. But I have the terrible feeling that like the married swingers I met, one partner, somewhere along the line, has made that compromise. I'll go along with it, they think, and he (or she) will come to really love me. And it won't matter, because he (or she) will change.

Silly women used to marry homosexuals, thinking the same thing. They never did change, of course. Neither did the folks who wanted to swing with other people's mates. And neither do sharks, in the boardroom or the bedroom.

Exes and Exits

Whenever my husband and my ex meet (and they do occasionally, the world shrinking daily as it does), they are exceedingly polite and overly warm to each other. There is a lot of firm handshaking, bright smiling, and an inordinate number of how-are-you's, just-great-thanks's, and how-have-you-been's. Anyone watching one of these courteous little encounters would be forgiven for thinking that here are two men who either (a) really like each other or (b) really despise each other. In fact, neither is true: Here are two men who do not know each other, but have in common excruciatingly intimate knowledge of a third party (me). It is not every day that one meets a stranger who has not only seen one's spouse naked, but may have also seen her naked, first thing in the morning, before she has had the time or presence of mind to suck in her stomach.

These days, almost every North American adult has an ex-spouse or ex-live-in-lover, and who among us would have it any other way? I would be a little suspicious of the adult without a past, who had never been involved or in love. Being the first — either sexually or emotionally — in someone else's life should matter only to fourteen-year-olds, for whom it may even be an attainable goal.

Still, although a marriage can be wiped out with a few strokes of a judge's pen, an ex does not simultaneously fall off the edge of the world, although it would be both appreciated and convenient. In fact, the very word "ex" suggests finality that for most of us does not exist. Rare is the person who never sees/runs into/hears about the ex. Indeed, some of us, because of The Children, are doomed to maintain reasonably civil ongoing relationships with our exes for ever.

Shared love and responsibility for children strikes me as the only acceptable reason to stay in touch with one's ex. I do not subscribe to the modern view that it is perfectly normal for two people who were once in love to remain interested in each other, to want to remain friends, to chat occasionally on the phone or, God forbid, meet for lunch once in a while. I would not take kindly to a late-night call from my husband's ex, even if she were in desperate straits and "had no one else to turn to". I would be unimpressed if she called him for advice, and I would buy a gun if she wanted to meet him.

I see it like this: I have no terrible memories of the man I was with before David; just the opposite, in fact. He was, and is, one of the nicest, kindest people I know. At the same time, I have no desire to see him, to look at pictures of his new wife and family. I would never presume to go to him in times of trouble, nor, I believe, would he come to me. We abdicated our right and obligation to do so when our relationship ended; besides, one would assume our need to turn to each other had disappeared sometime earlier.

A friend of mine had this sort of complicated relationship with her ex. Five years after they had parted, she still phoned him occasionally, deliberately drove past his house once in a while, and sent him cheery Christmas and birthday greetings. On the surface, her reasoning made sense: "I still *care* about Michael, Christie"; or, "It's the anniversary of his father's death, and I just want him to know I'm thinking of him"; or, "Michael's so good with stocks, he'll advise me what to buy". But deep down she knew, and I knew, she was really trying to re-establish a connection. She was involved with someone else, and so was he, but she wanted to know that somewhere out there, there was the ex, still pining a little for her, still treasuring the time they had had together, still thinking of her as his Number-One love.

Another friend, who had always prided herself on her maturity, who claimed not to have a jealous bone in her body, was stunned when, out of the blue, her husband's first wife called him, sobbing on the phone, to see him the next day. The woman's second marriage had just collapsed, and she was devastated. She wanted, she said, to talk to Leslie about what she was doing wrong, about why none of her relationships lasted. My shaken friend was struggling with herself. "I suppose," she said, "it makes sense, because she and Leslie were so close for so long, and in a way, he does know her better than anyone else. I understand why she would come to him for comfort." At the same time, my friend was unnerved and strangely unsettled by the call.

"So is he going to meet her?" I asked.

"Yes, tonight."

"Where?"

"I don't know."

"YOU DON'T KNOW?" I screeched. "I'd be staking out the joint."

"Oh Christie," she said with a sad smile, "I can't do that. Leslie *has* to go."

In a pig's ear. If David ever got that kind of phone call, I wouldn't understand, let me tell you. And if the ex asked to meet him for drinks the next day, I would be on the extension, purring, "We'd love to come." WE, not him. It seems to me that if you can't muster up the energy to be protective of your marriage, if you don't care enough about it to feel at least a twinge of jealousy, neither will you give a hoot if you end up with another ex on your hands — him.

PART THREE: Bread and Butter

Mentoring

About a year ago, with a gnawing fear that I would begin using "network" as a verb and develop a briefcase, I was officially appointed somebody's mentor.

The somebody is an unusually attractive and poised fifteen-year-old. Her Toronto high school has implemented a "mentoring" program; the students, forced in Grade Eleven to decide What They Want To Be When They Grow Up, are sent out into the world to find a sympathetic body in their chosen field to show them the ropes. My young friend, smarter than most in that she recognized this so-called career choice was not carved in stone (despite what the school said), had an interest in journalism; and an acquaintance of mine who is an old pal of her father, approached me.

I long believed that "mentor" was Latin for "someone you have pictures of in a compromising position with a sheep". I also despise that it has become a buzzword, particularly among women, who pretend that "mentoring" is as natural a human female function as breastfeeding. Every bone in my body urged me to say no, so I said yes. Yes is always easier for me, which is why my parents were so fraught with worry when I began going out with boys.

I never regretted my answer for a moment, either, for my mentoree (mentoress? pupil?) is so bright and likable that time spent with her was a pleasure. When appropriate, she asked questions that showed an intelligent curiosity; when it wasn't, she sat quietly by my desk, watching me and my fellow reporters work (and managed to remain alert and awake). What few assignments I was able to suggest, she completed without my help and on time. She also had impeccable manners, rare in a teenager. I have no idea if she will end up in the newspaper business, but whatever she does, I know she will do it better than most of the world.

Though I believe most of us to be quite willing to help people in our businesses who are young or starting out, it is only in the self-important eighties that this normal befriending process would be given a pretentious name, built into our schools and management-training programs, etc., and lent a respectability and importance it does not deserve.

Despite what the newspaper and magazine advice columnists tell us, despite the quickie books that list Ten Easy Ways To Find A Mentor, and despite what the teachers at my young friend's school may think, a mentor is neither necessary to one's rise (be it to the top or the middle) nor someone one can get into one's corner by will alone. There are, I suspect, only a handful of naturally occurring mentor-protégé relationships, and they most often happen when unusually successful, driven people spot in young underlings the raw ambition and brains that they so admire in themselves. True "mentoring" is not a wise elder statesman taking a vulnerable young person under his wing. More commonly it is a form of self-recognition and self-love (Why, young Bill is as creative and energetic as I was at that age!) and an attempt to exert influence from the grave (And if Bill is president when I'm gone, it will be just as if I'm still in the big chair).

For most of us, "mentoring" is normal human kindness. We don't show X how to use the computer because it will be

Good For Her Career; we show her because we can't bear to see her struggle. We don't take Y out to lunch to meet our executive friends because They're Important and Could Be Good Contacts, we do it because we think they'll like one another; besides, if we leave the office one more time seeing Y eating a toasted western at his desk, we'll die of guilt.

When I was still a student, trying out for a job as a copy editor at *The Globe and Mail,* I was hired because some of the old pros on the desk claimed I could do the work. I couldn't, if the truth be known (though I learned reasonably quickly), but they lied and said I could. And they did it because they liked me. They weren't trying to be my mentors; they were trying to be my friends.

"Mentoring" is such a stupid word, especially as there's already a perfectly good one around: friendship. It can't be legislated — by high schools, or in management-by-objective sessions, or by well-intentioned heads of personnel. That silly "mentoring" program worked for me and my young friend because she's a smart, pleasant young woman and I liked her. And when she is the raving success I am sure she will be, I know that I will have had absolutely nothing to do with it (nor will any other mentors she is assigned along the way). The credit will be entirely hers, and that's as it should be.

The Eleventh Commandment

Once upon a time, when I was but a callow youth, I attempted to winkle a fat-cat salary out of a managing editor. I began by mentioning my immediate predecessor in the job, a man I shall call Dick Jones: "I happen to know that Dick Jones was making a lot more money in this job than I am." Gaining confidence, I cleared my throat and was about to continue when my managing editor interrupted me.

"First," he said, "it is none of your business what Dick Jones earned. Second, if he did earn more money, it is because he has been in this business for thirty-five years and has earned a fine reputation, which you, as yet, have not. Third, never, EVER compare yourself to someone else. Unless," he said, and it was he who was confident now, "you are prepared to suffer by comparison."

After the small raise of which I was worthy had been promised me, I walked out of that office, my face an unbecoming gray. I had learned my lesson and I have never forgotten it. Why had I not learned it earlier? All I can say is that I was quite young and very inexperienced.

I was, of course, also extremely greedy.

That was more than fifteen years ago, and my grasping arrogance in those days is obvious to me now, particularly my assumption that after only a year in the business, I was as good as any veteran and should be paid accordingly. What is just as obvious, however, is that there are not enough people like my managing editor to bring all the young snots into line. If there were, there would not now be so many bitter, resentful people stewing in so many offices, envious of the other guy's wage, or company-paid fringe benefits, or corner office. And surely, too, they would not expect, as a God-given right (just as they believe that somewhere in the repatriated constitution a person is guaranteed A Nice House and A Good Car and Maybe A Boat), an automatic annual raise, promotion, expense account, and paid overtime.

"I hear Bridget is going on that seminar in Florida . . . *again.*" "Why does *he* get a company car?"; "Can you believe he's just been put on the board?" There is a whine of, "Why not me?" in all that. Sometimes the *me* in question has a legitimate ax to grind (the office being no more fair than the world); but just as often he is only carping, making the mistake I made that day in the editor's office — comparing himself with others and assuming that because they theoretically do the same job, they do it equally well.

In recent years, government has gone so far as to incorporate this same self-serving assumption into official policy in the guise of "equal pay for equal work" and "equal pay for work of equal value". Equality of opportunity is a good thing; I am not made uncomfortable by governments or companies that advertise themselves as Equal Opportunity Employers. But "equal pay for work of equal value"? Hiring will become as complicated, as arbitrary, as subjective, and as petty as figure-skating judges who allot marks ranging from 4.5 to a near-perfect 5.9 for the same performance.

If there had been "equal pay for equal work" laws when I was trying to land myself that raise years ago, the managing editor would have had no real option but to give it to me. Dick Jones wrote five columns a week; so did I. My editor, perhaps, could have made some allowances for my lack of experience and seniority; but otherwise I would have had him cornered.

Don't think I wouldn't have liked the money. But the editor was right. I was doing the same job, but I wasn't worth as much — quite literally — to the newspaper as old Dick Jones had been: I didn't deserve the same wage. Learning this when I did has probably kept me from going crazy many times since, and is one of the reasons I have usually been unreasonably happy about my jobs, my employers, and my work life.

Thus the eleventh commandment — perhaps at the office, even the first: thou shalt not covet thy neighbor's paycheck.

The Women Who Would Be Queens

Every large office has one; certainly, every large office in which I have worked had one.

They are always female (I am not being sexist, I am being accurate), almost always young or youngish, reasonably bright, and usually pretty or, at the least, attractive in an outlandish way. But none of this is why you notice them (though attractive set off to advantage by ten inches of Spandex tube skirt may be what initially drew your attention) or why they are such a problem. I am referring to a few — not the vast majority, *not* even a sizable minority, but a few — of the breed that used to be collectively known as Secretaries. In this age, when titles are as important as salaries and even the guy who cleans your office in the dark of night is likely to carry a crisp stack of business cards, we call them Administrative Assistants or Executive Secretaries or Assistants To. But just ask them: Their duties are much the same as ever. They type (or word-process); they answer phones; they file things (usually in a system no one else can understand, which makes them invaluable; like I said, they're bright); they order couriers and mail clerks about with the efficiency that they also exhibit keeping supply cabinets filled with pens and letterhead, etc. And most of them do all this with uncommon grace and ease.

The exceptions — that mere handful — are The Women Who Would Be Queens, who, with wild illogic, regard the job as a way station on the road to stardom: being Discovered by Somebody for Something, or, at worst, Like, Being In Videos. They do not want to be Secretaries, or even Administrative Assistants. They do not want to type (and usually, they can't). They do not want to be there (which they so often aren't). And the thing they do not want to do more than all the other things they do not want to do is answer the fucking telephone.

A Queen can sit at a switchboard, every button on the thing lit up, and ignore every one of those flashing lights.

I once asked a Queen — just this once — to keep an eye on my line while I raced to the bathroom to relieve the immense pressure on my bladder. (It was the only thing I ever asked her, aside from, "So how do you want your coffee, Marla?", which I asked her every morning.) I am reliving the scene even as I write it: "I'm expecting a call from Ottawa, and I'm on deadline. But I've got to piss, so can you watch my phone for just a minute?" Nod from Marla. Wind sprint to the loo, brief sit down, wind sprint back: Elapsed time, forty-five seconds. Phone is ringing. "Hello, hello, HELLO!" I shout. Dial tone. "Marla! Marla! Why didn't you get my line?" Injured look from Marla. "Jeez, you don't have to get nasty."

I have seen a Queen leave unanswered 456 business calls, yet pick up the phone the one time it is her mother, with whom she spent the next thirty minutes talking, in whispers, in Ukrainian. (Another thing about Queens: even if they are White Anglo-Saxon Protestants, fifteenth-generation Canadian, they talk to their mothers in Ukrainian or Hungarian or Italian or Lithuanian — any language you cannot understand.)

I have known Queens whose philosophy about telephones was: If it is important, the person will call back (although no one would answer that call either). I have known Queens who thought the work ethic meant that if you get in late, you are entitled to leave early. I have known Queens who *functioned* in their Other Lives, who could do three dozen difficult things at the same time, who could make Cecil B. de Mille look like a ditherer but who could not find the Q on the typewriter keyboard in less than an uninterrupted hour.

The real problem with Queens, though, is getting rid of them, for they tend to be as charming as they are irritating. Just when you imagine that you have hardened your heart enough to complain and/or fire them, they will fix upon you an over-mascaraed gaze of immense vulnerability, and ask if you would help them out by, oh, introducing the members of their rock band at a charity concert, or writing a letter of reference to Robert Redford on their behalf ("You write so well"), or allowing them to take your picture for their portfolio of portrait photography, or reading their short story before they submit it in that contest. How, in the face of such cunning flattery, could anyone with a heart — or ego — ever complain. I couldn't. It may even get to the stage that I eventually found myself at with the aforementioned Marla.

"Marla," I said one day, having missed my seventeenth important call of the morning. "We have to work something out." And we did: I sat at Marla's switchboard, and answered the phones. She sat at my computer, polishing her latest short story.

You've got to be firm with a Woman Who Would Be Queen.

Boss Ladies

I have had several female bosses. One was a perpetually excited, demanding, and inspiring fireplug of a woman, who was generous in her praise, tough as nails when she had to be, and probably the best editor I have ever known. Another was a shy, nervous creature who was forever sacrificing her news judgment for whatever expedient and easy story she thought would be Good For Women. She probably ranks as my least favorite superior. A third was a reasonably astute and kind woman whom I liked very much, and who probably falls, as most of us do, somewhere in the middle.

Now would be the appropriate time and place to say that just as there are no characteristics peculiar to male superiors, so are there none to women bosses. I would very much like to say this, but I do not believe it to be true.

The obvious notwithstanding — that there are as many different sorts of male bosses as female ones — the two groups do, in my opinion, have qualities and operating styles that have much to do with their gender.

Take, for instance, the three women I have mentioned. Though they were as different as night and day, they had some common characteristics that I have never seen (or at least, not seen so vividly) in their male counterparts.

On a superficial level, all were exceedingly well-dressed —

far better dressed than their male peers. (This is not as impressive as it sounds. In the newspaper business men tend to short-sleeved shirts, so worn that their singlets show through, and shiny, baggy-assed pants.) The women also had better haircuts and wore more expensive fragrance. They scrupulously took their turn getting coffee for the gang; the male bosses merely took their turn paying, which is infinitely less troublesome. And not one of the women ever came into work smelling of booze, something I can say for few of the men who have been my bosses.

More important, all three women were lousy at office politics, and took all such gamesmanship, particularly when they were losing, very personally. They brooded more than the men, and saw conspiring cabals where a man — more accurately — would have seen only incompetence and mismanagement. They were much more reluctant than the men to discipline or fire anyone, preferring to gather files of damning evidence — for years, if need be — until the guilty party could be persuaded to take early retirement or be shuffled off to a less-demanding, but equally paid sideline.

The women were much better at handling people: they listened to their employees more, they worried about them more, they cared more, and the employees knew it or sensed it. Outside the confines of the office, it was a different story. The women ate and drank and socialized with their employees far less than the male bosses did. They seemed to be fearful of stepping over invisible boundaries, wary of mixing business and pleasure, nervous about starting friendships that might later blur the worker/management line that loomed like a Berlin Wall.

I hardly need add, but will, that many of the male executives were both indiscriminate and indiscreet about sleeping with femal underlings. If any of the three women dallied in the office, it was with other management types. I know because, like everyone else in the joint, I watched them more carefully than I ever watched any male boss, and no breath of a rumor ever sullied one of those shining female reputations.

Perhaps because of the distance they kept from their employees, the women were lonelier and more isolated and more insecure than the men, and any revelations about their own problems tended to come from out of left field, blurted (behind closed doors, blinds drawn) in great startling, sometimes sobbing rushes that left them embarrassed and you reeling because you'd had no hint that they might be unhappy. Troubled male bosses, in my experience, tended to leave such obvious trails — constant references to "the bitch" and sleepless nights spent on the office couch, increased drinking, occasional fistfights, much sighing, etc. — and suffered woe so blatantly and so self-indulgently that by the time they officially split with their wives or lost their jobs or were demoted or had their paychecks garnisheed or whatever, it was old news to most of the working stiffs.

Whereas the men were smart enough to grab their share of credit for things done well, the women were so careful to praise everyone else that their own involvement in any project could be easily overlooked. At the same time, they were less able to take criticism or blame when it was rightfully due them. Not, you understand, that they shifted the blame to anyone else; but they took it all as a personal affront — as if their judgment in general was being called into doubt, rather than their judgment in a particular instance. The women wanted to be liked, more than the men did; criticism is not easily borne by those who want to be universally adored.

There are undoubtedly exceptions to all these generalizations, but I have not known them. I think the woman boss is an entirely different breed than the man. I don't buy the feminist propaganda that women, being nurturers and mothers, are more compassionate or more intuitive, any more than I believe that because men have traditionally played team sports, they are better at winning at the office or better at keeping the office "team" together. But I sure as hell know that men and women make different bosses.

Anyone who is surprised to find that this is so might do

well to remember that old adage — "If my uncle had tits, he'd be my aunt."

He doesn't, and he wouldn't, and it's as true in the office as it is everywhere else: If Dagwood's boss, Mr. Dithers, had been Ms Dithers, Dagwood wouldn't have had all the problems he did. He would have had a whole set of new ones.

The Office as Cuckoo's Nest

I have seen it happen several times — once when I was traveling through Europe on an extended holiday, and again a couple of times when I have been covering Olympic Games in close quarters with hundreds of members of the international press.

In Italy, I found gesticulating, garrulous, espresso-drinking Italians who could have stepped out of a cartoon. In Paris, I found Frenchmen as haughty and as cool as any who might have inspired the old line about the city being a great one — except for the Parisiens. It seemed I went weeks in England without seeing a Limey who wasn't chinless and prone to saying "Right then!" and "Be a good lad". In Munich, the streets were crawling with red-cheeked, lager-swilling Germans dressed entirely in loden green up to their hats. At the 1988 Winter Games in Calgary, I watched in disbelief as, every day, in the cavernous press center the Americans turned ugly (not to mention, into aggressively patriotic flag-wavers), the Canadians wished even security guards barring their way to sites they had a perfect right to enter "a nice day", and the Japanese went around, video cams and cameras in hand, grinning cheerfully and taking endless film of the whole happy scene.

Trust me, a little, when I say that there is more than a grain of truth in most of our stereotypes. Moreover, we tend most often to become caricatures of ourselves: (a) when we are under stress; (b) when we are packed into small spaces; (c) when we are forced to spend too much time with people we don't know very well; and (d) when we can't easily get away from all of the above — in other words, when we are at work.

This may not be the only explanation for the vast number of bizarre characters who appear regularly in most of our offices, but it is surely among the most charitable. It is far gentler, I think, to write off the weird behavior of some of our fellow workers as the result of "pressure" or "environment" or "the lousy lights in this joint" than to admit what may very well be the truth, which is that they are wackos.

Is there, anywere in the world, an office of reasonable size that does NOT have:

The Organizer

Usually but not exclusively female, The Organizer is the person who pulls together the birthday parties (complete with balloons, hats, festive noisemakers, and appropriately decorated cake), wedding and baby showers, retirement fêtes, expressions of condolences (complete with flowers and maudlin cards), get-well wishes (complete with teddy-bear gifts and silly cards), singing telegrams and strip-o-grams, and all group activities or outings from New Year's party to Christmas lunch. She always brings the wine, wraps the presents, remembers the napkins and plastic cutlery (or volunteers to fetch same), cuts the cake into perfectly even pieces and passes it out, collects the dirty dishes, brings the camera and, worse, takes the damn pictures.

Invariably, she is described as "nice" or as having "a heart of gold". Almost invariably, she is, if not a raging incompetent, in a position far too exalted for her (which is why she does all the other stuff, her theory being that if she can't do the job she is paid to do, she will otherwise make herself indispensable). And there is no getting rid of her, because whenever you are tempted to punch out her lights, you ask yourself if you want to have to remember everyone's birthday and be in charge of tasteless cards and gifts.

The Nurse

I do not speak here of an RN, which some progressive-type companies have tucked away, but of the real nurse, the office nurse, The Nurse. Most often but not always a woman, The Nurse always carries: aspirin, Bufferin ("It's easier on the tummy"), Vitamin C, Tylenol and "something a little stronger"; penicillin, and for those who are allergic, a tetracycline alternative; Valium and a generic substitute; oil of cloves for toothaches; Tampax, Light Days, and extra-strength Kotex; bandages, gauze, adhesive and tensor wraps of various sizes; antibiotic cream; suntan lotion and a spray guaranteed to take the sting out of sunburn; dental floss, mouthwash, toothpaste and a spare toothbrush; for ulcers, Tagamet, Maalox, or Alka Seltzer; exotic massage oil, several condoms and a month's supply of birth-control pills, and for good measure, needles, thread and a goodly assortment of buttons.

What is annoying about The Nurse is not so much that she needs to be needed (which is a pain in the ass, but bearable), or that she likes to be begged ("Just how bad is that headache, honey?"), but rather that once she has dispensed a single tablet or drop to you, she will forever inquire about your health in loud, solicitous tones. She thinks of herself as The Doctor, and makes snap diagnoses about your condition ("It's your heart, isn't it?" or "That sore on your lip . . . might be herpes") and orders you to lie down. Still, you must never treat The Nurse unkindly, or you will be denied help come the next hangover. Never, however, see her for any ailment of a sensitive nature, for unlike her formally trained sisters, she has no sense of patient confidentiality.

The Einstein Gofer

Usually but not always male, and most often young, The Einstein Gofer may be your office boy, mail clerk, in-house courier, punching bag for the secretaries, errand-runner, or general all-round company toadie. (Every office needs a toadie or two.) The thing is, everyone but management knows this toadie is a genius. A better secretary than any secretary, a more pleasant receptionist, a finer manager than all the managers, a more gifted diplomat than the vice-president in charge of personnel, he is not only the only guy in the joint who can run the copier, he's the only guy in the joint who can fix the computer system after it's crashed. Usually, he's also engaging, personable, and wickedly bright. So why is he always making $11,500 a year, with no overtime pay, and getting coffee for people unworthy to lick his boots? Because everyone is scared to death that if the word gets out on the little SOB, it's *their* job the bright bastard will snare. Fret not: Once recognized, The Einstein Gofer usually rockets to the top. Unless you're the CEO, you needn't worry. Talk this kid up, promote him. When he's running the place, he'll remember you kindly.

The Simperer

Most often a female but sometimes a male homosexual, The Simperer always, always wishes you a good weekend on Fridays and then grills you on Mondays; approaches you at odd moments — you are on the phone, interviewing a client, or ensconced in a toilet stall — and asks, in somber tones, "Are you okay?". She giggles at all your jokes, even the bad ones, and then confides, "I don't get it"; gives you unasked-for weather reports; loves what you're wearing (even if you've been wearing it for a week); regularly inquires if you are "doing something different with your hair — it looks wonderful"; asks where you bought those fabulous shoes/gloves/earrings. She tells you how much she just loves your spouse, and always makes sure to get you a coffee, even when she's on her way to the loo, seven floors from the coffee machine. So, as they say in those little tests in the magazines, What's Wrong With This Picture?

What's wrong is that The Simperer doesn't do all this just for you, she does it for everyone — for people she likes and people she hates, for the office boy, the boss, and strangers who wander in from the street by mistake. She is, in short, wildly indiscriminate — not only a simperer, but a whore. Feel free to treat her badly; she will still treat you exactly as before. She will simper, and you will feel guilty.

The Good-Old-Boy Politician

Usually male and usually youngish, The Good-Old-Boy Politician is acutely sensitive to your position in the company. When you're hot, he will invite you home to dinner, get you invited to functions he deems important, send you memos that sing your praises, buy you lunch, phone you "just to talk", introduce you to his valuable friends, pat your dog and compliment your children. When you're on the skids (even if only because you were hot for a while), he doesn't know you. He won't return your calls, and neither will his friends; he's "booked solid" when you invite him to lunch or dinner; he takes the back stairs to avoid passing your desk; he becomes allergic to dogs and forgets you have children. There is no point in resenting this; The Good-Old-Boy Politician, lacking other survival skills, is merely protecting himself. He is also useful: by his actions, you may gauge your future in the company — and be certain of your present status. Use him as he uses you; the wonderful thing about The Good-Old-Boy Politician is that he is utterly impossible to offend.

The Loyal Old Dog/Stoolie

Male or female, young or not, The Loyal Old Dog/Stoolie usually resides in the office equivalent of protective custody, in a tiny corner of his own under the thumb of his immediate superior, to whom he tells all. Loyal Old takes the official company position on all matters and always toes the line; he loves his job, and announces this frequently; ditto for the boss and the firm. Any whine or bitch no matter how harmless — even a "fuck this joint" will suffice — from other employees is treasonous and immediately reported to his first-in-command. In short, he has all the less-than-noble qualities of both the average canine — he is pathetically grateful, inappropriately eager, mindlessly devoted, and blindly loyal — and the jailyard snitch — he squeals on his fellows with equal fervor, whether they have cursed the boss, stolen paper clips, or embezzled millions: You may be inclined to give him the occasional boot to the head, but remember that, more than anything else, he is an anachronism — a company servant in a time of merciless cutbacks; loyal in an era when loyalty goes largely unrewarded, when the paternalistic, benevolent company is long-gone. When all is said and done, The Loyal Old Dog/Stoolie, who sells his soul to the company, will be left like the rest of us, with a gold watch and a pension that doesn't go far enough. He may be worthy of your scorn, but he is also deserving of your sympathy and a little kindness.

The Lysol Lady

She is the genuine eccentric, the woman who brings to the office her own seat cushion (emblazoned with her name), her own pencils (to avoid those dangerously sucked-on or chewed by others), her own paper slippers (fresh ones every day), and her own mug and eating utensils. She may wear crisp white gloves whilst working or a newly washed linen handkerchief over her nose; before touching anything, she may spray it heartily with disinfectant. Very often, she will brush her teeth (and sometimes Water Pik them, too) eight or nine times a day. Certainly, she will put name tags on all personal property (including desk, chair, telephone, stationery, coatrack hook, filing cabinet) in the faint hope others will not touch same. She will, however, spray all of the above before each use. Anyone tempted to tease her (a single cough will turn her bowels to water) should watch The Lysol Lady at work: She may be madder than a hatter, but she is usually also stunningly efficient, once her assorted sanitary maneuvers are out of the way. And Lord knows, come Christmas, she's easy to shop for — a can of you-know-what and you've got a friend for life.

The bottom line is that in the office, as in the foreign country, people often seem so stereotypical as to be cartoon characters. In both cases, this is mostly because we never really get to know them, and are just passing through. If you're in Munich only one Sunday, the day folks dress up in their loden-green outfits, you won't see their working clothes, which are much like ours. If you see The Organizer only during office hours, when she's trying desperately to make herself useful, you won't know that she's also the competent, composed mother of three at home.

Add to all this the fact that the average office is not unlike the average airplane, a small, closed environment where you spend long hours in cramped quarters with imperfect strangers. Some of them drink excessively, fart wantonly, talk too much or too loudly, or exhibit other odd behaviors. The real wonder is how well most of us get along most of the time. The other real wonder is that while policemen have a catch-all word for violence that occurs in the home (the "domestic"), there is no comparable one for the office: I mean, is there a copper alive who has ever responded to a "bureaucratic"?

Big Brother, Big Business

A few years ago, the newspaper where I work instituted a health-incentive scheme that was widely hailed as progressive and farsighted. It was, perhaps, the only time such adjectives were applied to the *Toronto Sun* by the small-l liberals who wouldn't literally dirty their hands by reading "That Rag", as they call it.

Essentially, the deal offered employees cash bonuses to quit smoking or lose weight. The program began one New Year's Day and ended the next; if you had stayed weed-free for the duration, or lost and kept off weight, you got your money. The plan was, as I recall, quite successful.

I toyed briefly with giving it a shot myself. I may have quit smoking for a few hours and I distinctly remember hoping that by giving up one dish of ice cream a day (which still left me with two), I might accidentally lose a few pounds and be eligible for some greenbacks at year's end.

One of my reed-thin colleagues, infuriated that fatsos were being rewarded while health-conscious and slender people were not, deliberately shaved five or six pounds off her already bony frame just so she could collect some dough.

Anyway, neither my heart nor my stomach was in it, and I gave up. About a month after the official start of the program, however, I did quit smoking, falling just weeks short of qualifying for the cash bonus — a curious bit of timing that I think now was no coincidence. And a year after the program had come and gone, I joined Weight Watchers and lost forty pounds, which I am happily still without.

I am proud that I did both those things (I have since taken up smoking again) by myself, without having to carry a company flag. I am also quite smug about the fact that no one had to pay me to lose weight (au contraire, I paid Weight Watchers to help me).

I have rarely had so much fun at a job, and I have never worked for a company I like more than the *Sun;* however, I was offended by the Big Brother implications of the whole program, resentful that a corporate nose was being stuck where it has no business being, and insulted by thinly disguised bribery. I remain disturbed because I think it is the way of the future.

The North American business community has been told so often that a physically and mentally healthy employee is a more productive employee (not to mention, a cheaper one, given that the fit non-smoker is a better insurance risk and allegedly takes fewer sick days) that it has begun to believe it. There is a growing number of companies now embracing wholeheartedly the concept of "complete care for the complete employee".

Forward-looking firms may offer health schemes like the *Sun*'s, or pick up the cost of employees' night-school courses, stop-smoking clinics, and health-club memberships; even old-fashioned companies have drug and alcohol rehabilitation programs for employees. Some businesses, come expansion time, will incorporate their own fitness facilities in a new building; others sponsor basketball or hockey teams. A great many companies regularly send entire departments off for think-tank seminars or weekends at posh country inns; and the most stylish firms provide daycare for employees' children, so that Mum and Dad are not only worry-free, but also available for lunch-hour bonding.

I can see good in almost all of these so-called advances; but the problem is, they occur as a part of the "total care" package. In this future private-sector welfare state, an employee's every need is anticipated and met by the company, the ultimate Great Provider. Eventually, the employee becomes so sated and dependent he has neither the free will nor the desire to up and quit. Trading one's liberty and independence for creature comforts is a raw deal.

Three or four years ago, before my husband decided to make his hobby a career and become a full-time artist, he applied for a job as an analyst with a nationally known market-research firm. There were, I think, a half-dozen positions open at the time, and the competition for them was fierce — exams, tests (psychological and otherwise), a series of tough, tense interviews (one-on-ones, three-on-ones) with progressively senior company officials. With his training as an urban planner, and his head for statistics and logical thinking, and what I consider to be his considerable personal charm, David won one of the sought-after spots, and was promptly immersed in a six-month training program that was, we soon realized, equal parts brainwashing and company propaganda.

The rookie analysts were required to put in long days — in by 8:00 A.M., out, if they were lucky, by 8:00 P.M. with only a few hours' work still in their bulging briefcases. The shiny glass-and-steel complex was located in a northern suburb with few restaurants nearby, so the recruits, like everyone else, either ate in the cafeteria or went out in large, over-organized groups to "really get to know each other" and to "form a good team". They were soon invited to join the company's many sports teams, informed that the company would pick up the membership fee at the posh squash-and-fitness facility nearby; and exhorted to come out on the weekend to the company squash tournament or dance or hockey league. They were soon spending so much time together that they began to look alike; indeed, in the company uniform of tasteful, subdued suit and tie (both men and women) and sensible shoes, the white-faced, baggy-eyed, sleep-deprived trainees were interchangeable.

Within a month, one of the new recruits packed it in; the next month another. By the fourth month, though he was doing the work magnificently and was at the top of the class, David quit. By the end of the training period, only two of the original six were still with the firm, and one of those left about six months later. All of them, incidentally, had turned in more than satisfactory job performances, but walked out on a starting salary of about $30,000 a year and a list of perquisites as long as your arm.

The company is undoubtedly among the most progressive in its various employee programs and benefits; yet, for David, it was that pressure to make the office the center of one's life, to be part of a winning "team" — that turned him off the place. I suspect that to varying degrees, the others also suspected they had not only joined a new company, but were little by little surrendering control of their lives.

A friend of mine is an executive with another such "progressive" firm. Three or four times a year he spends the entire weekend at a splendid resort with the department he heads. These weekends are always highly structured: an early breakfast followed by workshops and seminars; a group lunch and "walk"; more workshops in the afternoon; a group dinner followed by a group "dialogue" or "round-table discussion" of the events of the day, and finally a group sing-song. (Everyone is urged to bring along guitars, etc.) Employees are bunked two or three to a large comfortable room, and their time is spoken for. (The only privacy they have are stolen moments spent in the john.)

Throughout the weekend, the employees are urged to get in touch with their feelings, engage in self-criticism, and confront their fellow workers. One such late-evening session ended, my friend told me, with a grave-faced discussion about organizing one's time, focusing on a physical description of the daybook each employee used, how he "broke up his day", and an explanation of why he was where he was every hour of every workday.

My friend intensely dislikes these weekends; other employees are no more keen than he is. Most would rather be with their families, at the cottage, at home, watching *Hockey Night in Canada,* getting drunk, whatever. Every so often someone suggests this, albeit more politely, to the powers-that-be; every time, they meet with a brick wall: It is good to clear the air, they are told. It is good to sit around with your co-workers, and really get to know them as people. The department that thrives together survives together. And every year, four more weekends are lost to the company.

I am not convinced there is anything Machiavellian about any of this; but I am sure that power surrendered is difficult to get back. Let anyone make a decision for you — a person, a government, even a company — and you may find you want to make fewer of them yourself. It may be good for your physical health to quit smoking or start working out, but when Acme Tool and Die offers you money or some incentive to do so, it cannot be good for your soul. It may be more convenient if your children spend their days at Acme's in-house daycare center, only two floors below your office; but when Acme wants you to work late, and the objection that you have to "get home to the kids" is removed, will you see more or less of them?

We all want good jobs, pleasant and safe working conditions, reasonable salaries and fringe benefits; but I think that is all we can ask of our employers. When they voluntarily offer us more, we should regard them with a jaundiced eye lest, in our hast and greed and laziness, we rush to say, "Yes, please."

If the company says, "Jump — it's for your own good", do

we reply, "How high?". We are giving up something rather precious, and, in the long run, it isn't for our own good, but for the company's.

No Sex Please, We're Colleagues

Our society seems endlessly fascinated by the fact that in the past decade, women have entered the work force in record numbers, broken into previously all-male dominions, and taken on, to use the politically correct but horrible phrase, all manner of "non-traditional jobs". We also do our damnedest to deny one of the most logical corollaries of this trend, which is more sex at the office.

Magazines proclaim our interest in the former — self-important headlines like "The Changing Face of the Work Place" and "Women and Power" introduces profiles on female construction workers and carpenters and legal eagles (all posed in appropriate gear, from steel-toed shoes and safety goggles to Harry Rosen pin-stripes) — and earnest books dispense advice to one sex on how to cope with the latter.

Yet, it is only in magazines like *Cosmopolitan,* with a reputation for spicy, slightly titillating, "not-her-real-name" reportage that the natural consequence of all this equal opportunity is addressed — albeit with breathless story titles and Helen Gurley Brown exclamation marks ("Good Girls DO!") that no one takes seriously.

Intra-office sex is nothing new, of course: Was Perry Mason really immune to Della Street's ample, sweater-clad charms? What fifties housewife didn't have a twinge of worry about hubby's pneumatic Personal Secretary? How many old-time standup comics built a career around the bitchy wife at home and the sweet young thing in the typing pool? When female employees were few, or in low-status jobs that left them open to the power-play aggression we now characterize as sexual harassment, we may not have faced the issue squarely, but at least we acknowledged its existence.

Now, however, with half the work force female, with more and more of us working closely with the opposite sex as equals (which tends to render any physical encounters consensual), we pretend it never happens — in spite of all the evidence that it bloody-well does. Who can't think of one set of co-workers who are carrying on? Who can honestly say they have never dressed with a little extra care to impress someone in their office? Who doesn't know of one colleague who left a spouse for a co-worker? Certainly in every office or snack bar, swimming pool, or newspaper I've ever worked, at least one of my fellows has been involved with another (sometimes, me). And yet, our popular literature reflects none of this.

Women, I think, are guiltier of this hear-no-evil, see-no-evil approach than men, particularly the new breed of career woman. She appears to believe that if she continues to deny, deny, deny (that client A is attractive; that she had a fling with colleague B; that colleagues C and D are sneaking out for unduly long lunch hours and everyone knows it), nothing will have happened. (It's a new twist on the "if a tree falls in the forest and no one hears it . . ." rationale.)

Certainly, in my experience, this is true of the new breed of female journalist. While carrying on a torrid affair with the police reporter, she churns out lengthy odes in praise of the eighties professional woman as being so businesslike, so efficient, so aware of the career risk of a damaged reputation that she is above it all. The female journalist never says this directly, of course, but her stories are full of innuendo: "Jane Smith, one of a handful of female private detectives, has given up all dreams of marriage, children — even a social life — to rise in her chosen field. . . ." "The crisply businesslike Mary Jones, dressed in a severe gray suit, says she has had no difficulty handling her twenty-five male colleagues . . ."

It's a pity that we go to such trouble to hide this stuff. After all, most office affairs don't end in shattered careers, just bruised egos. It is not impossible to have the hots for someone and still work effectively side by side. Besides, many intra-office attractions are never more than exciting but reasonably harmless flirting.

Whenever you get men and women in the same room for upwards of seven hours a day, you are going to also get some chemistry. Most of it will come to naught (except making work more interesting) and of the few full-blown affairs, only a fraction will result in a soap opera of broken homes and lost careers. Most people who fool around in the office, like most people who fool around anywhere, are young and unattached. The married ones who carry on at the office are the same ones who take off their wedding rings before entering a bar and deserve the trouble they usually find.

Sure, men and women *are* equal in the work place, but we sure as hell aren't the same. So why do we try to pretend that for a twenty-five-year-old man, working beside another twenty-five-year-old man is as exhilarating as working beside a twenty-five-year-old woman with legs, as my dad always said, right up to her rear? Or that for a young woman, working cheek-to-cheek with another woman is no less amusing than working with a lean young man whose suit cannot disguise his hard hockey-player's frame?

Give me a break. When the French say *vive la différence,* they don't add — "but not at the office".

Fast Times at Ridgemont Inc., or, Notes for the Ambitious

On smoking:

It used to be, smoking was not good for your health; now, smoking is not good for your career. Many firms advertise themselves as Smoke-Free Environments and hire non-smokers only. Soon a cigarette will be a ticket to a dead-end job. If you are a would-be fast tracker who smokes, you have two choices: (a) give it up, or (b) lie. Neither course of action should pose any difficulty for the rawly ambitious, most of whom are smart and rich enough to take up a more socially acceptable habit, like cocaine.

On drinking:

In the old days, a casual invite to "have a drink with the boss" was a sign that you were doing well, impressing the old sod. The modern equivalent is the invitation to a squash game. The same rules, however, apply. Just as the boss was the one to get drunk, he is the one who wins. Some things really never do change.

On sports:

Traditionally, employers have looked with special favor upon young men and women who played (or claim to have played) sports in high school or college. This is still true, but some sports are better than others. No one who is really ambitious admits to having played football anymore (too many head injuries), or hockey (too much violence), or wrestling (too much groin-grabbing and falling about). Boxing, despite its tendency to cause major brain damage, is very chic these days. (Look what a boxing background did to improve the overtly slick, over-packaged sheen of Ontario premier David Peterson's image. Voters felt they could trust a guy who'd gone toe-to-toe in the ring, and taken a few shots to the head. I figure the voters had taken a few too many shots to the head, but what do I know?) Running, golf, and soccer, all non-violent, non-contact games, also have cachet. This is because the companies that once looked for signs that an employee was good at team sports (and thus, "a player"), now search for clues of headstrong individuality (and thus, "a leader").

On personal stuff:

Admitting that you are in a drug rehabilitation program is cool; joining Alcoholics Anonymous is not. Some criminal records are okay (drug-trafficking, student-loan fraud); others are not (a drunk-driving conviction is terribly uncool). Gamblers Anonymous is perfectly acceptable, Overeaters

Anonymous or Weight Watchers are considered disgusting. Regular sessions with a psychiatrist or therapist is quite all right; meetings with a financial counsellor (especially a court-appointed one) is quite another. Confessing you got your first job at your daddy's company is by no means a no-no but is not as modern as getting your first job at your wife's firm. Speaking of wives, a career-woman wife is a definite asset; a stay-at-home type is a hindrance. The acceptable compromise is the wife who Does Charity Things. It is "honest" and "open" to admit you've had a face lift, breast implants, tummy tucks, and almost any other plastic surgery, but 'fess up to a toupee or Hair Club membership at your peril. Being Jewish or Catholic is quite In; being Protestant isn't; but nothing is quite so hot as being a born-again Christian. This is particularly good for the fast-tracker, as becoming one takes no study or time; just Opening One's Heart To The Lord.

On politics:

Clever young employees with an eye on the executive suite used to join the political party favored by their firm. These days, this is career suicide; because even old, traditional firms change their political stripes as often as most of us change socks. There are two ways out: join no political party and claim allegiance to the one in favor at the moment. Or join them all, which gives you the same maneuverability and a nicer tax deduction.

Big Sir

We live, alas, in increasingly egalitarian times.

I say alas because while I agree that man and woman are equal, as are black and white, Hindu and Jew, Irish Catholic and Irish Protestant, homosexual and heterosexual, and so on and so on, I have a little trouble with the concept of boss and employee as equals. They aren't.

The boss has the nice office, the good salary, the expense account, and most important, the power to put you on the graveyard shift for the rest of your natural life. These are not criteria that lead normally to friendship, yet, as the old social boundaries grow increasingly blurred, more and more of us are having this very thing forced upon us.

Frankly, I liked it better the old way. You called your superior Mister or Sir. At closing time, you went your way and he went his, and the only time you met socially was at the annual company party — and then, only for the ritual handshake and exchange of greetings because you were both uncomfortable, you being dressed up and he being dressed down. Today, ambitious employees dress so well you can hardly tell who's who, and lowly you may even have to dance with the boss's spouse — my ultimate definition of stress.

It is made more confusing by the fact that many of us have several layers of bosses. There's our immediate superior, with whom we can sometimes relax and behave in a reasonably normal fashion. Then there are middle managers, with whom we shouldn't let down our guard; they are all fighting for the top spots and it makes them untrustworthy. Finally, there's the Boss of Bosses, the company president or CEO, who is very often the nicest of all, but with whom it is difficult to relate, as his suit costs just less than your house.

(My Boss of Bosses at the *Sun* is the immensely affable Doug Creighton, the man who founded the paper, oversaw its aggressive, unprecedented growth throughout Canada and the United States, and is now president of the entire chain. I like him very much, and have long harbored the urge to go drinking with him, get wildly drunk, and tell him how I would run his newspaper. But this would be tricky, I think, with someone I cannot address by his first name. "Hello, Sir," I say whenever I see him in the newsroom. "For Christ's sake, call me Doug," he once replied. The next time he passed by my desk, I said, "Hello, Sir Doug," and that's how I've addressed him ever since, much, I suspect, to his chagrin.)

Over the years, several of my various bosses have subscribed to this new equality business and attempted to become friends with me and David. Disaster.

Once, when I was in a new job at a new newspaper, a senior executive invited us to her exceedingly posh home for an exceedingly posh dinner with some of her exceedingly posh friends. Now, this was a big deal for David and me, as our normal social life revolves around hockey games, televised and live. By the time we arrived, we were as nervous as two pedophiles in the exercise yard with the general prison population.

She met us at the door of the gracious old mansion, and as we walked into the glamorous foyer, David grinned and said smoothly, "Nice lobby." We drank to excess and I was the only smoker at the table. Near the end of the evening, our hostess asked after our large, black, mutty dog, who usually went everywhere with us.

"Oh, he's in the car outside," I said.

"Bring him in!" our hostess exclaimed.

"Oh, he's fine," I said. "He likes it there."

"I insist," she said, "just bring him in for a minute to see Pookie and Pickey [her small, well-behaved, purebred something-or-others]."

Finally, we relented. David went out to fetch Blux, who made it as far as the verandah before relieving himself at length on what I am certain was an exquisite antique. Pookie and Pickey were unimpressed. We left, half-snackered and giggling loudly, as dog urine ran down the leg of the chair. Oddly, we were never invited back.

Another highly placed executive took a shine to us, and for about a month, we were bombarded with invitations: to his private club for a party; to drop in for a drink; to go nightclubbing with him and his friends; to his house for dinner. Wisely, we weaseled out of most of them, but on two occasions, I failed to come up with plausible excuses, and we were doomed. The party at his club was with all his non-office friends, most of them, like him, members of a certain political party. David and I distinguished ourselves by picking fights with every single one of them. We criticized everything about the political party, especially its leader, for whom many of those in the room had campaigned. At midnight, whirling about the dance floor, David suggested either we leave immediately or he would be throwing up on the hardwood. We left.

The other event was a dinner at the man's house. David was reasonably well-behaved, but I won the admiration of all. First I insisted that the host play only the three records that I liked out of his collection of three thousand. Then I took to dancing on his valuable old dining-room chairs and singing, in memory of my late father, filthy airforce songs. Each time I mounted a chair, my host would let me dance a while, then gently lead me away, tucking the chair in under the table. Seconds later, I would pull the chair out again, and repeat the performance. That, suffice to say, put the kibosh on any future invitations, and I'm sure he was as relieved as we were.

Neither David nor I is shy and retiring; but we do not normally engage in hostile acts, in friendly territory. I am at a loss as to why we behaved the way we did (and no doubt will again) when being courted by my bosses. And yet I know we are not alone: I remember well fist-fights and pie-throwing incidents when other employees were forced into socializing with the brass.

The only explanation I can think of is that we're not really in friendly territory, but in a demilitarized zone where a cease-fire has been arbitrarily imposed. I have liked most of my bosses, and I don't for a minute believe I'm "not as good as them, wot?" But I think there is something unnatural about trying to be pals with the guy who's going to decide your raise next month.

Besides, if truth be told, I'm not sure I *want* to be friends with people who would rather spend Saturday night chatting than watching *Hockey Night in Canada*.

Day Terrors

One of my friends has worked for the same company for eight years; I have been at the *Sun* for little more than six. In our circle, we are considered to be veritable rocks, islands of serenity in the storm. Most of my friends, and most of those in the generation immediately behind us, change jobs (and companies and cities and even careers) with a regularity that would have scared the pants off anyone who learned the value of a steady paycheck by doing without one during the Depression.

One of my friends moved, within a five-year period, from Toronto to Vancouver to Toronto to Montreal; another moved from a daily newspaper in Ottawa to regional-level television reporting in Regina to a job as a national TV reporter in Montreal, in eight years. A third left a cushy job as a hotel publicist for starvation as a freelance consultant, then to a new career in real estate and, when that didn't work out, part-time jobs as a typist. My husband moved from urban planning to advertising copywriting to a brief stint as a statistical analyst to his current status as modern Jack-of-all-trades — full-time artist, part-time hockey-rink Zamboni driver, free-lance cartoonist, and amateur home renovator — in about five years.

On the surface of it, all this moving would suggest we are also a fairly fearless bunch — packing up ourselves, and sometimes the family, at a moment's notice, unafraid to take chances and try new things. But I suspect most of us are scared to death, at least some of the time.

There are few things so unsettling as a new office: Where's the bathroom? What floor is the cafeteria on? How often do we get paid? What am I going to do for lunch? Who are all these people? What are the rules, written and unwritten?

I have gruesome memories of my first two weeks at the *Toronto Star;* I'd come from *The Globe and Mail* to an ill-defined, nebulous position as a columnist. No one, including me and the man who had hired me, had any real idea of what I was to do, and all of us were too polite to say so. I was assigned a desk in the vast *Star* newsroom, and for the next fourteen days I just sat there, typing The Quick Brown Fox Jumped . . ., and Now Is The Time For All Good Men . . . over and over, just to fill the awful blankness of the paper in front of me. Too embarrassed to look up, too shy to talk to anyone, too self-conscious to do anything but sit there, I sweated so profusely I destroyed the underarms of everything I wore. At the end of two weeks, I slunk to the city editor's office and begged for an assignment. He obliged, and in another two weeks, I was back on my feet, not so cocky maybe, but confident enough to look my new colleagues in the eye.

Entrances and exits are a necessary tool of the trade for most of us, a skill never needed by our fathers and grandfathers, who made the company quarter-century club before they knew it, who changed "careers" only when economic conditions left them no choice. We need to know how to leave and how to start again. With companies taking over other companies that five years ago took over other companies, we need to know how to move in and move on gracefully, so that when we run up against a former employer in a new guise, we are not doomed by our history.

Leave-taking is, I think, the simpler exercise, assuming you don't burn any bridges, by badmouthing the boss, the company, The Job, the pay. If they're nice enough to throw you a goodbye party, you can stay reasonably sober and make an innocuous speech (if a genuinely pleasant one is beyond you). If you harbor resentment, keep it to yourself; go gently, so that come takeovers or mergers or just the ever-shrinking business world, you'll be able to work for and with those people again.

The graceful entrance is trickier. If you come in (and why else would you have moved?) as a glamour puss, savior, or high-paid hotshot from the competition (or from Toronto), most of your new colleagues will be predisposed to dislike you, on principle. They think you got the job someone else was in line for; they assume you're making more money than they are. You may find yourself managing a group of people who are older and more experienced than you are.

Go slowly. Don't try to be friends with everyone the first day, and for God's sake, don't buy the whole office coffee on your first morning; they won't respect you by the afternoon. Get the lay of the land: figure out who's who and memorize a few names; find a toilet that you like; do all the things, except cry, that you did on your first day of school. If there's a bar popular with your new co-workers, stay out of it until you're given an invite.

If you take it nice and slow, by the time you've figured out whose nose is out of joint, it won't matter so much. Most of all, don't go to your new quarters until you've got a lot of work to do; don't do what I did, and spend days wandering about getting panic-stricken. If you're working hard, you won't care if you eat lunch at your desk; if other people see you working hard, they're more likely to ask you to come out with them.

And remember, however scared or unnerved you may be, the key, in the immortal words of every aerobics instructor who ever lived, is to "Keep breathing! Keep breathing!" It's the only thing to do until you've settled in. All the rest, in time, will follow.

On the Firing Line

I was fired once.

When I was a teenager, I worked as a supervisor in a children's playground. I didn't feel like working one day, phoned in sick, and headed off to my local swimming pool to bask in the sun. An hour or so later, one of my bosses spotted me merrily doing cannonballs off the diving board. That night, I got a call telling me to report to his office the next day. I did, and was regretfully fired by this very nice man, a friend of my father's who found the experience excruciating. I felt ashamed and guilty for the rest of the summer, even though I lined up two other part-time jobs and my parents eventually, reluctantly, forgave me.

It seems almost quaint now, like those apocryphal stories that started "When I was your age, I used to walk five miles to school every day". Who, for heaven's sake, walks five miles to school now? And who ever gets fired? Plants close, and people are suddenly out of work, sure; there are cutbacks in certain industries, and employees are temporarily laid off, or work from week to week without knowing how long it will last. But who gets fired?

Today's rare firing is not a thing cleanly done, as was mine, and there is no element of finality to it. It is a new beginning — time to launch the lawsuit, time to claim wrongful dismissal, time to get the application for unemployment insurance. The half-dozen people I know who were fired in the past decade were never so busy, so driven, as they were in the weeks immediately following their firings. If they'd worked half as hard at their jobs as they did at setting the legal wheels in motion, they would never have been canned in the first place.

The easy answer is to blame the unions, who have bargained into their contracts increasing protection for their members, squarely placing the burden of proof on the employer — where it belongs. For a firing should not be a simple process, subject to the whim of a company or a manager. I don't recall hearing of many instances where a union-won protection unduly handcuffed an employer from dismissing an employee who deserved to be fired — except, of course, for the federal post office. There, it seems, inside workers' quirks such as fire-setting, destruction of property, and drunkenness are prerequisites for being hired.

Management will often cite "the union" or "the guild" as the reason why X is still on the payroll; but in my experience, that's simply not true. More often, an incompetent or slothful manager, too lazy to document the case properly, is to blame.

At a newspaper where I used to work there was a veteran reporter, then in his early thirties, who had two serious and well-known problems: One, he liked the bottle rather too much; and two, his reporting was untrustworthy.

Reporters are used to hearing "But I didn't say that" complaints from people they have quoted: how stark quotes can look in the black and white of print in the cold light of day. If a source has seriously misjudged the impact of his words, he is likely to deny them or at least claim he was "quoted out of context". Yet, when you press him a little he will usually admit that he was quoted accurately, and his complaint boils down to semantics — whether he said "it is likely" or "it is probable".

But with reporter X, the complaints were of a different nature: When his sources complained that they had been misquoted, they stuck to their guns all the way to the press council or the courts. Some denied being interviewed by X; others said X had twisted their words or confused what they said with what someone else must have said. A few said they had never met him. The problem was a recurring one, and was growing worse; and everyone in the newsroom — including the managers and editors — was aware of it.

Several times the paper did the right thing and got professional help for X's drinking problem. Yet no one moved on the equally serious problem of his reporting. When he could no longer be trusted to handle major assignments he was shuffled off to features. To my knowledge, he was never disciplined.

His downfall came much later, when, once again, his star had risen despite his reputation. He was assigned a fairly important story, and was caught in the act of making up interviews, complete with fictitious names, bogus quotes, and non-existent case histories. With apparent reluctance, and after much debate, he was finally given the boot — only to reappear at the same newspaper, months later, as a freelancer.

He should have been fired years earlier. That he wasn't had nothing to do with the union, and everything to do with a management team that saw fit to protect him. Neither, in my opinion, should he have got freelance work from that newspaper — at least until he had redeemed his reputation by producing work of reasonable quality somewhere else.

None of this, of course, is peculiar to the newspaper industry.

Take the case of Y. He is a very bright middle-aged man with a pair of impressive degrees and all sorts of senior-executive-level experience. A few years ago, he did a stint of unemployment, during which time he received UIC benefits although he'd left his previous employment voluntarily, and with a sizable golden handshake. (He also had a sizable bit of family money). He then accepted a new position that involved a fair amount of travel. Almost immediately, however, he decided he didn't want to travel, and searched for ways to get out of it. Soon, in fact, he decided he didn't like the job, period, and would phone in ill a day or two a week. He did have his eye on a position held by someone else, however, and began angling for that. The company realized he was unhappy, offered him several lateral transfers, all of which he refused; in due course, he was fired.

Well, sort of: He promptly hired a lawyer, who promptly filed a claim of wrongful dismissal, which the company promptly settled out of court. Six months after he had taken the job, he was considerably richer and able to take another extensive vacation, during which time he reapplied — successfully — for unemployment benefits.

Or take Z, who turned down her company's bid to transfer her — not to another city or to another kind of job, just to a different job. This move was perfectly in keeping with the firm's longstanding and well-known tradition of moving its people around every three or four years. It was, also, a genuine promotion. She refused the move. The company made her another offer, which she also refused. After half a year she was fired.

Well, sort of: She, too, got herself a legal man, and he fired off some letters of intent, and before you could say Jack-the-bear, she was a year's salary richer.

I can think, off hand, of several other cases of employees — who were out-and-out negligent, or hopelessly incompetent, or so shiftless as to be utterly useless — all of whom were allowed to "leave" their companies, sizable and undeserved settlements in hand, when they should have been shown the door. I can think of a dozen more who have the collective work ethic of a fat old dog on a hot July day, and all of them are still gainfully employed.

The reason this concerns me is because I believe it is the indirect cause of the lousy service I get in a restaurant; the bored indifference of the sales clerk who won't ring up my purchase until she has finished nattering on the phone to her boyfriend; the bad job done on the brakes of my car; the sloppy, shallow reporting I read in the magazines; the shrug from the dry cleaner who has lost my blouse; the inaccuracies in invoices I am sent.

It is, I know, a cry in the wasteland, doomed to fall on deaf ears. But how are we to learn that, as my daddy always said, a job worth doing is worth doing well (and worth showing up for, and worth working at, and worth trying to master) if the people who do the job badly are never disciplined or fired?

When I was canned so many years ago for lying about being sick, I felt degraded, like a lousy slacker, which is precisely how I should have felt. I expect that today the boss who saw me doing cannonballs off that diving board would look away and pretend he saw nothing, and I would get off scot-free. Or if he did try to fire me (the nerve!), I would threaten to go to court and assorted human-rights commissions, and he would cave in. I would be allowed to stay or would walk out the door, severance pay in my pocket.

And the lesson I would have learned is that mediocrity pays. The customer comes last; the skim milk rises to the middle, if not the top. And, oh yes, screw the system.

Well, fuck them: In my day, we WALKED the five miles to school.

PART FOUR: Professional Help

The My Generation

It was in the seventies, I think, that some clever soul (why do I have the haunting fear he was either an ad man or a writer for *Time*?) named us the Me Generation — that self-directed, self-absorbed, self-centered bunch who belatedly entered adulthood with a collective case of terminal cuteness and a child's fascination with gazing at ourselves in the mirror. Labeling us was nothing new (although this one hurt); in fact, our greatest single characteristic, and the one that will probably become our most infamous legacy, is our penchant for amusing monikers: Baby Boomers, hippies, Yippies, Yuppies, etc. The worst are the acronyms (DINKS — Double Income, No Kids), which lend themselves to catchy headlines and magazine covers (showing, of course, pictures of US).

In this tradition then, let me bestow on us yet another nickname. This one is for the eighties (the decade in which we approach our earning peaks) and for the grown-up status to which we are only inching.

We are no longer the Me Generation, we are the My Generation.

We're no longer interested in discovering who we are or where we're from or even where we're going. Fair enough: If we still don't know, after ashrams and drugs and gurus, tranquility tanks and aerobics, vegetarianism and nouvelle cuisine, we never will. But what we *are* keenly curious about is what we can buy, and where it's from — an impoverished village in Tibet or Guatemala? a cunning store in Milano? a bazaar in Afghanistan — and where it's going, i.e., over the couch on the long wall? by the CD player? in the solarium?

The cycle is complete: Once known for dropping (acid), popping (pills), bopping (around), stopping (wars), and copping (out), we now are known for shopping.

So many of us now buy so many of the same things that we have meaningless generic, shorthand that we all understand: Houses and cars come "with all the bells and whistles" or "all the toys"; kitchens and bathrooms are "state of the art". Perfectly good nouns like "windows" and "jeans" and "sneakers" have been replaced by "Pella" and "Edwins" and "Reeboks" — brand names that pass as real words.

But we also buy (or, in some cases, rent) people and expertise, and once bought and paid for, we consider them to be as completely and surely Ours as we do when we bring a rug home from the store. It is not unusual or inconceivable that a typical middle-class single adult would, at any given time, have in his or her employ as many as a dozen people whose first names are all "My" — My Psychiatrist, My Hairdresser, My Cleaning Lady, My Butcher, etc., etc. We get married, they change their name and multiply: Our Renovator, Our Decorator, Our Therapist, Our Caterer, and so on. Add a couple of little ones, and you're into the big numbers: Our Housekeeper, Our Nanny, Our Allergist. . . . Well, you get the idea. The nuclear family (Mommy, Daddy, and 2.5 kiddies) has, forgive the expression, mushroomed beyond belief.

Our fathers did their taxes; we hire accountants; our mothers raised us with the expert guidance of their mothers and Dr. Spock; we go to pre- and post-natal classes, read how-to books, and call in counselors, consultants, and care-givers at the first hint of trouble.

The easy and not inaccurate explanations (that the tax system is now more complicated and today's world is a scarier place in which to bring up children) aren't the only ones. Somewhere along the line, in our pursuit of nice things and clothes and cars, we seem also to have bought the belief that we can hire all the expertise we will ever need to get us through life's crises. We shop for people the way others used to shop for a couch.

Take figure-skater Brian Orser. At the '88 Winter Olympics Orser was pitted against his longstanding American rival, Brian Boitano. Orser is a likable young man; but he decided a year or two back that he was frightened of winning. (Once he hid in the showers while Boitano was skating so he wouldn't have to hear the cheers of the crowd.)

In Calgary, Orser assembled one of the best "corners" in the history of amateur sport. In addition to the usual stable of helpers, Orser had his personal psychiatrist, whom he saw daily ("How do you *want* to feel today?"), his own "rolfer", who specialized in a controversial deep-massage therapy, his own nutritionist, and his own public-relations flak to deal with interview requests. Boitano had his coach and a choreographer.

In the much-touted "Battle of the Brians", Orser fell apart when he most needed to stay together. Despite all his precautions, despite the expertise with which he had surrounded himself, despite the genuine warmth and best wishes of everyone on "Team Orser", when push came to shove, Orser had to do the skating, and Boitano won.

Maybe it just wasn't Orser's night, as often happens in sport. But there's a hard lesson in there for the rest of us, which is that no matter how many experts we acquire, no matter how much advice we can buy, sometime we all end up on the ice alone, usually when it matters most. We would do well to remember it.

Modern Slaves

A friend of mine, who shall remain nameless, was once a ghost. She wrote, unofficially and for money, one of those how-to-succeed, how-to-be fabulous books, which treat with humorless gravity such burning issues as starting your own guppy farm and the right eyeshadow for blondes.

Her alleged author was a minor TV celebrity whose sun had long since set, but who managed — through tenacity and the well-placed connections of the affluent man in her life — to shine in the social columns, described as a "well-known broadcaster and journalist". (Several years have passed, but the "author" is still shining as such, with cloudy intervals, though she hasn't appeared on the tube regularly in a decade and was never, ever a journalist.)

Sunshine's contribution to the book that bore her name was twofold: She talked into a tape recorder and later sent the tape to my friend for transcribing, and she allowed my friend to come to her fashionable home to "interview" her.

At the time, my friend was doing a very eighties' balancing act — managing full-time motherhood and part-time, free-lance magazine and newspaper writing. On any normal day, she could be found wiping noses, driving her children to kindergarten or music classes, trying to knock off a column or two, making dinner, taking her mother downtown, and trying to find five minutes to spend with her husband. Like most, she did it with very little help — a baby-sitter two mornings a week so she could write with minimal distractions. Her wardrobe leaned to sweatshirts stained with strained prunes, and on a rare evening out with her husband she considered it a great victory if she got her contact lenses to stay in her red-veined eyes for more than half an hour.

Frazzled and preoccupied, she arrived at her author's plush home about nine in the morning. She was greeted at the door by a submissive Hispanic maid, ushered into the living room kept spotless by the housekeeper, and offered tea and croissants. Moments later, the author appeared, in the latest color-coordinated Danskin, her hair a big, stylish mane. Sweating lightly and tastefully, she introduced her "trainer", the fitness instructor who came to the house three or four days a week to put her through a designer workout. Then, as my friend took notes, her tape recorder running, the author talked for an hour or so about the difficulty of being a "working woman", before lunch and a whirlpool at her club. Sometimes, they would leave the house together, my friend fighting with the door of her beat-up station wagon, the author dressed to the nines, slipping behind the wheel of her BMW.

All this tried my friend's patience greatly, particularly as the author took several southern vacations in the course of the writing because she couldn't "deal with the stress". But more than anything else, it is a nice illustration of life on the current version of the Mississippi plantation — which is to say, the reasonably affluent, white, upper-middle-class home.

Now, I am not suggesting that we should never employ people to work in our homes. There are as many of us who need the help as there are those who need the work. But there are ways of dealing with people in our employ, especially when they live among us. One can assume Sunshine's haughty, mistress-of-the-mansion attitude or one can behave, as does a friend of mine, with ordinary civility and kindness. My friend's help consists of twice-a-month, half-day visits to her condominium by a middle-aged housecleaner. The woman is well-paid, trusted with a key, thanked for her work, and in ten years of working for my friend, has never had to ask for a raise. My friend gets an automatic annual pay hike, so does the cleaning lady. The first time, the woman was so taken aback she immediately blurted out that (a) she hated asking for more money, and (b) my friend was the only client from whom she had never had to ask for a raise. (The woman was so grateful that ever since, my embarrassed friend has been fighting a losing battle with her *not* to do her ironing.)

I am not talking here about an employer's legal obligations: domestics are beginning to be protected against exploitation and unfair wages. I am not even talking about moral obligations, such tricky matters as not taking advantage of live-in help (easy to do because, after all, they're right there), and not unconsciously stretching job descriptions (e.g., asking a nanny to do up the dishes) to suit you. What worries me, I suppose, is the unlegislatable stuff — making sure we treat those who work in our homes with common decency, dignity, and respect. What really galled my ghostwriter friend (aside from the fact that she couldn't afford all the help that the glamorous Sunshine could) was the cavalier and peremptory manner with which Sunshine ordered about the Hispanic maid. Lord knows (and so did my friend) that maid did more good, honest work than Sunshine ever did.

Strangeness in the Night

One night, near the end of a long drive home, I begged my husband to search out something interesting on the radio to keep us alert. After much dialing about, he found one of those phone-in-for-sex-advice shows, and what we heard was a better stimulant than a direct hit of caffeine into a major artery — anguished voices (most, but not all, teenaged) describing intriguing problems in lurid detail.

The most riveting of these conversations was between the solicitous host of the show and a young man of nineteen who had two complaints: he had a small spot on his penis, and every time he and his girlfriend made love, she bled profusely.

This was gripping, all right, but what really grabbed our attention was the peculiar sense of urgency shared by the host and the young man. Their conversation went something like this:

Caller: "Yeah, like I was wondering if it's, like, normal for a girl to bleed all the time when she has sex?"

Host: "Are you talking about menstrual blood here? When your girlfriend has her period?"

Caller: "No, like, it's every time we have sex . . . . I mean, you know, we have it, and it's pretty good, and then she always bleeds from . . ."

Host: "The vagina?"

Caller: "Uh huh. I was wondering, you know, if it could have anything to do with . . . . well, I have this little red mark on my . . . on my . . ."

Host: "Your penis?"

Caller: "Yeah, on my penis, and I was wondering, like, if that could be what's making her bleed all the time? Like, there's a lot of blood . . ."

Host: "How big is this mark on your penis? Can you describe it *exactly* for me?"

Caller: "Well, you know, it's just a little mark . . ."

Host: "Can you look at the spot *right now* and tell me *exactly* what you see?"

Caller: "Okay, uh, it's . . . it's right at the end of my pen . . . penis, and it's really little, eh, it's a little red spot . . . and . . ."

Host: "Does it cause you any pain? Does it itch? Has the spot changed color recently?"

Caller: "No, no, it doesn't hurt or nothing. It's just there. Just a red spot, like a pimple or something . . ."

Host: "How long has it been there? When did you notice it first; can you remember?"

Caller: "Just a few days, I think. I mean, it hasn't been there a long time or nothing . . . Does it sound serious or what?"

Host: "I can't tell you that, caller, but just to put your mind at ease, I would urge you to make an appointment *tomorrow* with your doctor and have it checked out. Okay?"

Caller: "Uh, okay. And what about my girlfriend who bleeds all the time . . ."

Host: "I'm sorry, I've got to move onto another call. Thanks for phoning the Sex Advice Show. We'll be back after this commercial."

And sure enough, after a cheery plug for a smokeless, cigaretless world and the "Break Free!" jingle, she took another call, leaving us doing mental first-aid on the poor girl. It reinforced my natural reservations about *ever* phoning such a show for advice and, I suspect, also sent David to the bathroom to hunt for suspicious red marks. Still, I can understand the appeal of those faceless, disembodied voices that are flourishing on the airwaves, dispensing advice on everything from sex to real estate to gardening to doctoring to buying a used car to, well, sex.

First of all, anonymity is virtually guaranteed: Callers are always identified only as "Mike from North Van" or "Danielle from Pointe Claire". Everyone uses fake names and sometimes even fake, high-pitched voices — a sensible precaution, as you never can tell who's listening. All of which makes it easy to admit that you have never had an orgasm, or were had in a land swindle, or bought an absolute lemon. Moreover, there are a great many folks out there in Radioland who have legitimate problems and no one to talk to. It is also undeniable that most people are curious about how they sound on radio. (This is why the first words out of the host's mouth are either "Can you turn down your radio please?" or "Have you got your radio on?". OF COURSE people have their radios on; they want to hear their own voices.)

Such shows undoubtedly do some good and help some people, particularly teenagers who have, incredibly, managed to remain naive about sex and sexuality. Yet they seem a peculiarly modern option. Traditionally, if you had a medical problem, you saw a doctor; a money problem, you saw your bank manager — or loan shark; a legal problem, you saw a lawyer. Only in the media-saturated eighties do you don a pseudonym and talk to a voice on the radio whose only qualification for the job may be that she has a pleasant, well-modulated way of speaking, a sympathetic manner, and the ability to engross herself immediately in a caller's problem.

I mean, I'm sure that that young man raced to the doctor the day after he called to get the spot on his penis checked out, but for all I know, the poor girlfriend may have long since bled to death.

Creepy Weepers and Other Funeral Faces

Before my father died, he had been sick, off and on, for years: He'd had emphysema for a decade, had been fighting cancer for about eighteen months, and endured one heart attack and two bouts of major chest surgery. He had been through chemotherapy and radiation, and became so frail that sometimes it hurt just to look at him. Even so, when he went into hospital for the last time, I don't think any of us were ready for him to die. A large part of me, I know, clung to the belief that he would come through it all, as he had done so many times before, with flying colors and the thumbs-up signal he always gave us. I think he knew he was dying, perhaps he had even grudgingly accepted it; but I didn't, and neither did most of those who knew him. No matter how sick or old or pain-wracked someone you love is, it is never the right time to let him go.

And as we are never ready for death — the shock and grief and the strange feeling of surprise — neither are we prepared for the death-dealers — the undertakers, the folks at the morgue, the government bureaucrats who want their forms filled in, all those soothing, solicitously determined voices.

My father's "funeral" was so painful that, even now, I remember few details about it. But it was also wonderful, because there was no funeral, not really. Rancid had given my brother strict instructions on what was to happen. He had ordered a party — at the banquet hall adjacent to the hockey rink he'd managed for almost twenty years, with lots of booze and food, and no flowers, no wreaths, no hint of religion, and no speeches. He wanted his friends to come and have a last drink on him, raise their glasses in farewell, and be done with it — very much in keeping with his straightforward, sacrilegious nature.

Most funerals, though, are not like my father's. In my experience, they fall into three categories, each with its own peculiar cast of characters and codes of behavior. We might as well familiarize ourselves with some of their finer points.

The White Anglo-Saxon Protestant or WASP funeral

Mourners should expect to be greeted and ushered about by pale, pasty-looking, hooded-eyed men in black clothes that are usually just a shade too short in the arm or tight across the chest. These fellows are attached to the funeral home, and include the mortician and assorted helpers, who may resemble minor-league hoodlums. They meet you in the parking lot, drive your car into its place in the cortege, decorate it with tiny funeral flags, seat you in the chapel or special grieving rooms, and direct the pallbearers. They speak to you rarely; but when they do, they refer to the deceased as The Loved One in voices deep and appropriately serious.

Inside the funeral home, there may be an organ; if so, there will be a tiny, elderly woman sitting in front of it. (It may always be the *same* tiny, elderly woman for all I know. God knows, they all look alike: gray hair in a neat bun, they sit straight-backed on their stools, swaying slightly as they get rocking.) She will not speak at all.

The minister does speak although he may not have known the deceased. He will make great generalized statements about there being a reason for everything, and a time for everything that are usually only personalized with the deceased's name (occasionally wrong). Later, after the actual burial, the mourners are usually invited back to a family member's home, where they stand about in uneasy groups, eating small sandwiches, sipping sherry, and avoiding the topic of death.

The Non-WASP Funeral

I call this one the Irish-Italian funeral, though it is not peculiar to these two ethnic groups. It is much more colorful than its WASP counterpart.

For several days before the funeral, family members "sit" at the funeral parlor, there to welcome friends who come to call and say goodbye to the deceased. The coffins at Irish-Italian funerals are usually open; if not, there is a black-edged photo of the late whomever atop the casket. There may also be a separate arrangement of photos, either by the coffin or in albums, which detail the deceased's life. Mourners are expected to look at everything with great interest; it is good form to stare — at the body, at the pictures — and to praise the flowers and choice of caskets; it is exceptional good form to touch the body.

The actual service is most often held in a church, complete with mass and hymn-singing and communion and sometimes a eulogy. Those attending should book at least half a day for the church.

Events at graveside vary, but usually include most of the following: The sequential shoveling of dirt onto the grave by family members including at least one young child who nearly falls in; the tossing of the deceased's favorite flowers into the grave as the casket is lowered; much wailing and breastbeating; and, last but certainly not least, the leaping onto the casket by a family member. Do not be alarmed; it is standard practice. No Irish-Italian funeral is complete without it.

Mourners eventually retreat to the safety of a family member's home; there, however, unlike the WASPs, they get broodingly drunk. There may also be dancing.

The Modern Funeral

This is perhaps the most heavily choreographed of the three. All the mourners have taken Coping With Grief courses, and know Elisabeth Kübler-Ross's stages of grieving inside out. They are determined to "break through the pain" and "work through the grief". At all locations (funeral parlor, church, graveside, wake, etc.), professional handlers are in attendance — doctors, counselors, psychiatrists, nurses, or those who enjoy mourning and cry easily. Such people, with the family's blessing, move smoothly about stroking brows, clasping hands, and forcing everyone to talk about the deceased and his death — and to cry. If you are not visibly weeping within fifteen minutes of entering, you will find one of these folks hovering, face creased in a smile of infinite understanding and sweetness. You'll hear "You'll really miss Larry, won't you? He loved you so". A hand will rub your back or give you a gentle massage, then, "Let go, let go of it — it's healthier". This is your cue to break into sobs. My advice is, unless you want one of the creepy-weepers to follow you about all night, do it.

Do not be surprised if you hear people refer to the deceased's death as "beautiful" or "peaceful" or "an awesome experience". On your departure, the family is likely to thank you for "sharing in Larry's death" and being "such a great support". It is, I think, all a bizarre offshoot of the hospice movement, which is fairly new to North America. Its laudable aim is to make death and dying as pleasant, natural, and comfortable as possible. Its strange side-effect is that some people take it too far. They try, with their relentless back-patting and exhortations to "work it through", to turn grief and mourning into an insignificant process that should take no longer than an afternoon. Death may be natural, but so is fear and pain; and neither can be exorcised in a few hours, no matter how healthy that might be.

The modern funeral is typical Baby Boomer behavior. When we were young, we'd "never trust anyone over thirty". By thirty-one, we began to worship middle age, to sing the praises of experience, of older women and mature men. Now that we are edging inexorably closer to facing our own mortality, we are trying to relate to Death as a friend. Good for those who can do it, I suppose, but let me say here and now, he ain't no friend of mine.

Why Plumbers Should Earn More than Doctors

There is a widespread belief, especially in the medical profession, that plumbers make more money than doctors. I haven't a clue if it's true, but I think it should be. Here's why:

1. Plumbers make house calls. Ha, you scoff. How could a plumber unclog your sink if he didn't come to see it? Ha yourself! He could do what the average doctor does when faced with, say, a clogged nose, which is to urge you to bring it to his office. The plumber could try to talk you and your sink out of acting up. ("What's this about your sink, Mrs. Anderson? The water won't go down? Are you sure? . . . Try this: Put two tablespoons of Drano in the darn thing, and leave it alone. If it still isn't working call me in the morning.") Or he may try to convince you it's all in your mind.

2. Plumbers have answering services or machines. If you leave a message, they will generally call you back. Doctors have receptionists-cum-rogue-nurses whose sole purpose in life is to protect their man in white from sick people. Unless you can imitate a death rattle, the receptionist-cum-rogue-nurse will sneer at your symptoms, tell you Doctor is tied up, and urge you to make an appointment next month. If you insist on leaving a message, she will relay it, minimizing your symptoms so he will feel no need to call you back, or double book his day so he will not have a chance to do so.

3. A plumber will not have as his first line of advice, whether your complaint is a flooded basement or a loose

washer, to quit smoking. A doctor will, even if you have consulted him for a torn ligament.

Understanding the Renovator

It speaks volumes for modern life that the most complex, demanding, and stressful relationship you are likely to have these days is not with your spouse or parents or even your in-laws, but with your Renovator.

As in all high-tension relationships, the power rests with one party. On the surface of it, as you are writing the checks he cashes, that party would seem to be you; it isn't. As much as the Renovator might need your money, you need his expertise far more. He knows this, and you will soon learn it. If you needed him only a little when your house was still intact, you need him dearly now that the downstairs walls have been demolished. You will need him even more desperately once he has cut the hole in the second floor where the new staircase will go.

The client-Renovator relationship is further complicated by several other factors beyond your control. The first is the nature of the Renovator. Not for nothing, is he self-employed. He enjoys the freedom of coming and going as he pleases (which may translate into arriving late and leaving early or only working Sundays), and the joy of "working with his hands" (on the golf course as often as in your house). He also does not take direction. Make the adjustment.

A friend of mine hired a Renovator to do over her kitchen and paint her house. She tried to fight the freelancer in him: She expected him there at 8:00 A.M., before she left for work; he arrived when he felt like it. She expected daily progress reports, oral or written; he saw progress as self-evident. By the end of their first week together, she began to leave little notes on those yellow, sticky-backed, tear-off memo pads.

When she thought he was going to do the cupboards, she'd leave notes all over the kitchen: "White cupboards, gray trim"; "Plain white handles here". When she thought he would be painting the bedroom, she'd leave the notes there: "Scrape windowsill before painting, please"; "Don't forget to use drop sheets for floors". One day, she came home to find all his gear packed up and gone, the work a third done. When she finally tracked him down by phone a few days later, he said he would not be returning — even though the money she'd paid up front didn't begin to cover the work he'd done. "You're driving me crazy, lady," he said.

What she had forgotten, of course, was that if the Renovator were the nine-to-five type, he would be in a nine-to-five business, wearing a suit. He isn't, and he doesn't. My husband and I learned this early on: We hired a Renovator who worked in fierce, manic bursts (he would arrive about noon and work straight through to midnight, drywalling anything that wasn't nailed down) or not at all (he would show up after two or three days' absence with a splendid tan). But at the end of any given week, he would have logged a minimum of forty hours. Who were we to suggest he do it in five eight-hour days?

There is a complicating factor: Renovators (and carpenters, painters, roofers, and handymen) are easily influenced by the weather. We once had a Renovator who didn't show up when it was raining, it was threatening to rain, or there was rain in the five-day forecast. Another liked to work on rainy days; pleasant, sunny days were for the golf course. A third wouldn't come if it was raining or fine; we quickly learned to pray for warm, dry, overcast days. Every Renovator is different, so you'll have to make a careful study of what weather attracts and repels him.

A third factor to be considered is that even though, on paper, you, the client, are to be made happy, in practice, it is the Renovator's state of mind that is paramount. If he isn't happy working for you or in your house, the odds are that you will never be happy with his work or your house. This is why you will be groveling before your Renovator, trying to please him.

My husband and I once hired a Renovator to convert part of our large slum building into an apartment. This apartment, I should tell you, was to bring in rent, on which we were counting heavily to pay our very first mortgage payment. As the deadline loomed, he was preparing to install a toilet when he realized he had neglected to buy a gasket seal. We promptly volunteered to dash over to the hardware store, promising to be back within half an hour. As we were walking to the car, my husband said, "Do you think he'll be there when we get back?" "I don't know," I said, having learned that Renovators do not like to sit about, idle, for more than five minutes.

David promptly did a U-turn, dashed upstairs to the fridge, and grabbed a couple of cold beers. These, he carefully offered to the Renovator.

As we made our way back to the car, he said, "Here we are, paying him by the hour, going out to get a part *he* forgot, and trying to lure him to stay put by feeding him beer." Then he made submissive bowing and scraping motions and all but rolled over on his back, like a foolish, eager dog before its master.

Ironically, the very qualities — this independence, stubbornness, pride, etc. — that make the typical Renovator an impossible employee also make him a wonderful friend. It is no coincidence, I think, that virtually every time my husband and I have hired a Renovator, we have ended up with a new friend. Our first, who went into the consulting business, drops by to talk hockey with us just as he did when he was working for us. The second stays in touch by phone, which is more than he did when he was working for us. The third not only fixed up that rental apartment for us, he moved into it and has become one of our closest and most valued friends.

Still, you can't be too careful. So whenever you leave your Renovator alone, make sure there's cold beer within easy reach. Just in case.

When Not to Call a Psychiatrist

I have absolutely nothing against psychiatrists, except that some people regard them as a necessity for full eighties living, like a microwave or a built-in central vacuum. Others turn to them whenever they are in the normal human condition, feeling slightly lousy. Still others, too lazy for self-examination, need them to point out self-evident truths. None of this is the psychiatrist's fault, of course, so when I say I have nothing against psychiatrists, I mean it. It's their patients who make me crazy.

Many people I know are seeing psychiatrists. Most were seeing them when we first met, years ago. Bets are, ten years hence, they will still be seeing them. Yet only one of those people — a manic-depressive, who will be taking Lithium for the rest of her life, and who, with courage and her psychiatrist's help, has learned to manage her illness effectively — only one, has been diagnosed as suffering from a specific mental illness. The rest can lay claim only to such modern conditions as depression, the blues, mid-life crisis, stress, or "burnout".

One woman I know saw her first psychiatrist when her first marriage broke up. The shrink's couch was apparently more agreeable than the marriage bed; by the time her second marriage ended, a decade later, she was on her fourth psychiatrist.

A man began seeing a psychiatrist when, after growing bored in his job, he fooled around with someone in his office, got caught in flagrante delicto and nearly lost his marriage. His wife wanted him back, but only, she said, if he got "some professional help". Soon, he was coming home from the shrink mouthing such platitudes as, "I've never learned to get in touch with my feelings" and "I don't really know who I am". She regarded this as a great victory: he was getting to the root of the problem. I regarded it as a great waste of money: he was ignoring the root of the problem, which was his lifelong admiration for long-legged women much his junior.

Another friend began seeing a psychiatrist because she wanted to break her chronic over-dependence on whatever man was in her life at any time. She ended up so dependent on the psychiatrist that she booked her annual holidays when he did, so she'd miss only two weeks of sessions, not four. An acquaintance began seeing a psychiatrist when, after a series of affairs with colleagues over three years, during which she badly neglected her two teenage children and doctor-husband, the marriage finally died. "I can't handle the guilt," she said. The way I look at it, the guilt was normal; going to a psychiatrist to get rid of it was not.

There are, in other words, many more times you do *not* need a psychiatrist than there are when you do: You do not need a psychiatrist if you are feeling lonely and want a friendly shoulder to cry on; you need a friend. Friends are the people who listen and pat your back and tell you you're swell — and do it for free. Psychiatrists charge for the same services.

You do not need a psychiatrist if you are suffering some vague undefined gloominess. This is probably not Depression, but even if it is, it is likely the normal kind that hits you out of the blue, for no reason, and makes you black and moody for a few days. The best cure — forgive me for sounding like my Protestant ancestors — is hard work or physical exercise — something that demands the skills of the body, and leaves the mind alone to heal.

You do not need a psychiatrist if you are grief-stricken after someone close to you has died. You are supposed to feel miserable. What you need is time. It takes a while, but eventually, it really does get easier. Telling a perfect stranger that you feel awful because a friend has passed away will not make you feel better; telling another friend how you feel might.

You do not need a psychiatrist if you feel guilty or embarrassed with good reason. If you have behaved like a schmuck, guilt is the price. No psychiatrist, no matter how well-regarded, can take away guilt that is deserved. What you need is to try to make amends. Old medicine, but it works.

You do not need a psychiatrist if you feel stressed. Almost everything about life is stressful, from running out of coffee to a big board meeting to cleaning out the cat's litter box. And no one, not even a shrink, can teach you how to "handle" stress; you either do or you don't. When you're under the gun you don't need to lie on someone else's fake leather couch; you need to lie down on your own bed and sleep for a while.

You may need a psychiatrist if you are feeling suicidal or homicidal (although I'm not entirely sure about the latter: Aren't there times when it's perfectly normal to feel a little murderous?), or if you are hearing voices or in the grips of a depression that won't go away. The black days, periods of anger, self-pity, loneliness, and fear are, alas, just part and parcel of being human. And there's not a doctor in the world who has a cure for that.

The Need for Lumberyard Advocates

Think of all the useless services there are — from personal shoppers, rent-a-bodies who will stand in the Christmas rush in your stead, to the folks who place swatch after swatch of cloth against your cheek to determine if you are a Winter or a Spring. I am, therefore, greatly annoyed and frankly astonished that there are still no companies hiring out guides to tour innocents through lumberyards, building-supply stores, and other bastions of hard-rock masculinity.

It isn't just women who are intimidated by these places. Men are, too: men who don't earn their living laying bricks, men who don't know drywall from Durabond, men who piss in toilets rather than against concrete pillars in unfinished buildings.

Lumberyards and the like are crying out for some management consultant or service pro to come in and take charge. These places are designed for construction workers, laborers, hardhats, not for you and me.

You go in looking to buy some wood. You manage to get in the right lineup, find a clerk who speaks English, order and pay for your wood. You are then left trying to figure out where to pick it up. If you ask, all anyone will tell you is, "Inna back." They will not tell you how to get there (usually, via secret laneways); they will not tell you which of the loading-dock areas to use (usually, the one where the saw is going full-tilt); they will not tell you how to spot the employees (who are indistinguishable from most customers); and they will certainly not tell you, until you have loaded all ten tons of wood onto your tiny car and the shock absorbers go into shock, you could have had the wood delivered for a small fee.

Now, if only you could hire an advocate to handle this kind of thing, just as the chronically ill are urged to hire advocates to fight for better treatment and their rights.

The Lumberyard Advocate would be young, able to speak both Italian and Portuguese (the working languages of most lumberyards), aggressively masculine (i.e., given to shouting "Yo!", high-fiving it, and strutting) and familiar with both the technical language of the order desk and the color coding of the wood "inna back". Either for a flat fee or on an hourly basis, a Lumberyard Advocate would be well worth the expense.

Just imagine, no more worrying that as you order your pressure-treated, clear, number-one cedar two by fours, your voice will crack girlishly; no more fear that the regulars will just know your construction boots aren't steel-toed; no more being tempted to apologize for not being at home with seven children. And no more taking a number, like the sign at the order desk says, and standing around for an hour while every

Johnny-come-lately gets served before you do, then finally complaining in a loud voice, only to hear: "We don't use numbers. The stupid machine's been broken for three years." I'd pay a lot not to go through that again.

Choosing a Real Estate Agent

David and I bought our first house the way most people buy a sweater, and with about as much thought. It was the only house we looked at. We hadn't been planning to buy, but a friend alerted us to this steal of a deal (the only house we could begin to afford) so we went to look. We didn't get a very good look, either, because the elderly Italian gentleman who owned it had the extended family over for dinner, and we felt we were intruding. What we really got was an impression of the place: small, lots of ceramic tile, kind of cute. Without the seventeen Italians, it would probably be plenty big enough, too.

Moe, the real estate agent, thought he'd died and gone to heaven. No, we didn't want to see anything else. No, we didn't have any questions. Well, one — where do we sign? We didn't quibble over the price, we didn't worry about its odd location (in someone else's backyard — we should have worried). "We'll take it," we said. "I've got one you might like better about a block away . . ." "Moe," we said again. "We like it. We'll take it."

I don't expect Moe made such an easy sale before or since. And, although we wouldn't have guessed it at the time, Moe, who seemed the classic sleazy, aggressive real estate agent, right down to the ingratiating whine in his voice, creases and cigarette burnholes in his suit, and tired gray stubble on his face, later looked pretty good to us, too.

About two years later, for reasons we cannot now remember, we bought the large slum building in which we now live and put our sweet house up for sale. We turned to a woman I shall call Tanya, an acquaintance, a friend of a friend; and she was the exact opposite of Moe. She was a TV-ad real estate agent — slick, polished, professional, well-dressed and accessorized. She breezed into our house, confided that she was best at the "warm fuzzies" — which is how she described the people-handling side of her job, talking up the folks, etc. — and was out again with the signed listing agreement before you could say Yves St. Laurent.

Tanya arranged a few open houses (which allow your neighbors to come poking about your home), placed a few ads, and fielded a few inquiries. "Have you had a lot of calls about the open house?" I'd ask. "Enough," she'd say, "but we'll see where we net out." Net out? Tanya was always waiting to see how things would net out, even as it became increasingly clear to David and me that our net was coming back empty.

Then little things began to go wrong: a series of ads never appeared; return phone calls to potential buyers were never made. And, of course, we could never reach Tanya. She was never at her company office, never at home. Later, we learned she was working at another job most days, typing. If she'd explained this to us, we might have been more understanding; but we grew so frustrated that we finally decided to fire her. Except, of course, we couldn't reach her. You don't fire someone, even a Tanya, via a message on the answering machine.

About a month later, Tanya forced our hand, announcing, on one day's notice, that she was going to England for a holiday. Would we mind awfully if she just passed over our listing to another chap in the office? Yes, we said, we did mind. We sold the stupid house privately, within a week.

The point of all this is not to complain about Tanya (though, I confess, that feels awfully good) or even about real estate agents. There are good ones and bad ones, as there are in any profession, and I'd bet in roughly the same numbers that occur everywhere else.

But in the eighties, when we tend to form opinions about people based on how they look and what they wear and who they know, it's nice to remember that it was Moe who came out smelling like a rose. Moe the slob, with the spaniel eyes and the ever-present butt, and the shiny pants, was twice the real estate agent that slick, smooth, slippery Tanya could ever be.

Never judge a schnook by its cover, that's what I always say.

Commercial Relations

It's the combination of the big-city housing crisis and my house-hungry generation that's doing it. Either that or the moon's been full for far too long. Why else are so many otherwise normal people becoming landlords? Without renting out a flat or the basement, many of us would soon have to face what we knew in our hearts all along — we can't afford the darn house. It is a role fraught with problems and pain; yet, as the house prices continue to rise, more and more of us are adding the cruel landlord's cap to the dozens of hats we already wear. Armed with the landlord-and-tenant regulations and a vague understanding that the heat must be on fall through spring, we jump feet-first into the business of renting accommodation to imperfect strangers.

Shortly after we acquired our slum building, my husband and I got our Renovator (whom you met earlier) to rejuvenate a tired coachhouse apartment over our garage, so we could put the thing on the rental market. We envisioned our future tenant as a slightly upscale, reasonably affluent, arty type who would adore and appreciate our yummy Yuppie touches — the cunning pot lights with dimmer switches for intimate dining, the high-tech outdoor light fixtures, the black-and-white ceramic tiles in kitchen and bath, the white-on-white cupboards, the tasteful dull wall-to-wall carpet, the doors we'd painted bright yellow. Our wildest hope was that we might be lucky enough to entice a quiet gay man with an eye for interior design.

We had a few urban sophisticates through the place, but our first serious inquiry came from an unlikely trio of middle-aged Maritimers — a couple and their slightly younger male friend — who arrived on our doorstep with first and last month's rent in cash, announcing that they loved the apartment. "We'll take it," they chorused. "But you haven't seen it yet," we said. "Okay, but I can tell you right now, we like it," they said. And sure enough, after a brief tour — how long can it take to show a small one-bedroom flat — they liked it.

Now, they weren't quite what we had in mind: She was only seven or eight years older than me, but worn so thin and gray after a lifetime of hard physical work (she was a housekeeper by trade) she could have passed as my mother. Her husband was a jolly, gregarious fellow with an immense paunch and such a strong accent (New Brunswick, we thought) we could hardly understand a word he said. The friend seemed a little simple — he had the air of someone who had been institutionalized for some time.

We were trying to do things by the book, so we handed them an application form (the woman filled it out, answering about a third of the questions in a childlike scrawl) and told them we'd have to check out their references. Like the trio themselves, these were questionable: Their former landlord said they were good tenants, the hospital where she worked acknowledged only that she was a "reliable" employee, the younger man was unemployed, and the older one mumbled the name of the company where he allegedly worked, but we didn't catch it and were too shy to ask again. The rent we were asking was about $150 a month more than their current rent, which was troubling, and we were concerned that the apartment was simply too small for three adults. They swore it wasn't.

Probably we should have turned them down, but we were a little smitten by them — from a third-floor window, we'd watched them leave, three odd-looking characters, all chain-smoking, all wearing serviceable but old clothes, shuffling down the street. A night or two later, leases in hand, we stopped by their apartment to have them sign the papers, found their quarters reasonably clean if sparsely furnished, and that weekend, they moved in. They were, true to their word, quiet, peaceful tenants who just liked, as they said, "to have dinner and watch some tee-vee".

Two weeks later, however, we were over at their flat to fix a leaky faucet, and learned that the older man had hurt his back and was off work. (We remained unconvinced that he had been working.) The younger man (in the same clothes he was wearing when we met him; we never did see him in anything else) was still not working at all, and the woman was carrying the entire burden on her frail shoulders. The first rent check was four days late; we felt so bad for them that we ended up splitting their heating bill, though it had been part of the agreement that they would pay it. By the end of the second month, she had also lost her job (though they didn't tell us until later), and there was no way on God's green earth they could pay the rent. When it was a week overdue, we finally phoned them. "Well," I said, feeling like an ogre, "we can't wait very much longer . . ." "I know," said the woman. "But these things happen, eh, and there's nothing we can do about it. I guess you'd better give us our notice."

With great reluctance, we did just that — on the proper, government-required form, pursuant to section X. We knocked timidly on the door, and down the stairs all three of them came, to stand with us outside on the patio. As we gave them the form, lightning flashed and it began to pour — perfect bad-movie symbolism for the mess they were in and the way we felt.

They had almost a month to find another place or a job, and perhaps they tried; but they weren't really equipped for the big city. The one job we know they went after was for a live-in couple to act as superintendent in a small building. It would have been a nice setup for them, we thought. But instead of the couple going for an interview, they sent their friend. He returned very excited about their prospects, and said they would find out for sure in a week if they'd got the position. We didn't want to send them packing — and possibly ruin their big chance — so they gave us the name and number of the woman who'd done the interview, and we called her. She was quite impressed with their references, but, "I'm hiring a couple, and I can't hire them until I meet them." We gently suggested the man and wife make an appointment, and let them stay another week in the faint hope they'd see the woman, get the job, and be back on their feet.

The week came and went. They never did make it down for the interview; they didn't get the job. And finally, we told them they'd have to leave. And they did, leaving nothing behind but a heavy film of cigarette smoke on the once-white walls.

We couldn't, of course, have felt as awful as they did (none of them could look us in the eye, their shame was so real), although we probably came pretty close. But of all the lessons we could have learned from this — to be more ruthless in tenant selection, to check references more thoroughly, to overcome our embarrassment at asking for such details as employer's name and number, etc. — the only one that hit home was that, like most people, we did not have the right stuff to be landlords.

This was one time we should have been more eighties and turned to the professionals — a real estate company or property-management firm with a businesslike attitude and skills. Too late, we learned you need a hard heart to be a landlord — and a stomach tough enough to take the sight of those three figures shuffling off into the night, down on their luck and terribly embarrassed, or the brains to look away. Take it from us: There's no such animal as cut-and-dried "commercial relations" when you're dealing with one of your own.

Care-Givers

In Toronto, hired "nannies" are such a fixture that real estate ads regularly showcase not the inground swimming pool, or the eat-in kitchen, or the fabulous greenhouse, but the "self-contained nanny's apartment". Sometimes to childless outsiders like me, it seems the primary concern of people having children is, Who Will Raise Them? We childless outsiders would rather ask, So Why Have Them in the First Place?

I realize, of course, that I am being a little unfair, and that there are perfectly good reasons for nannies — two-career families, women refusing to do all the childrearing, the economic necessity for both parents to work, etc. Yet even so, I can't help but wonder if there has ever before been a generation so casual with its offspring.

A woman I know typifies what I mean:

She and her husband have three children, under the age of six. He is an engineer, she a writer; their combined salaries have been stretched to provide a swish house in Forest Hill, two late-model cars, memberships in two expensive sports clubs, fashionable clothes, all the chic toys (a home computer, CD player, etc.), a cottage, a nice winter vacation every year — and, of course, a nanny.

Since the woman's first maternity leave ended, they have had a nanny. Some have lived in the spacious "nanny's quarters" in the basement; some "live out" and come five days a week. Now that there are three youngsters, the family's routine is well in place: The parents get up about six, spend ninety minutes with the kids before the nanny arrives, shower, eat, and are out the door until six or seven that night, at which point they spend another ninety minutes with the kids before tucking them in bed. One or two of the children are in various forms of kindergarten or pre-kindergarten; the nanny takes them and picks them up. Ditto for swimming classes, music lessons, etc.

About two years ago, the woman was offered a freelance-writing project of such importance that she took a leave of absence from her regular job. She arranged to work on the special project at the home of one of her in-laws. Although the children would often be in school or at class, and the nanny would keep them from getting under foot, if she worked at home, she said, "they might distract" her.

So for the duration of the special project, she spent a brief period with the kids before heading off each morning to the "writing house", as she called it, returning sometimes as late as nine at night.

The woman is forever displaying their pictures (they are extremely cute kids), buying them sweet little outfits (which she shows everyone at her office), and talking about how, when she is out of town on assignment, she misses them terribly. I'm sure, in her own way, she quite loves them. But I can't figure out how she knows she loves them, or what she thinks they're like. It takes a lot of hours to build a relationship with another human being, particularly with a child: How could she know?

I once wrote a column about daycare in which I interviewed experts who believed it was good for children as young as six months and those who believed it wasn't good, period. I interviewed a former colleague, who had stayed home with her two children only for the duration of her maternity leave, placed them in daycare, and argued that it was all for the good of her kids. When I asked her what she meant, she said it allowed her to provide a better quality of life for them. If she didn't work, they would not be living in a fine old Toronto neighborhood in a big house. They would have to live in a smaller house, perhaps in an area that wasn't as safe.

I was unconvinced: The benefits of that particular two-career family accrued primarily, it seemed to me, to the parents. They wanted the nice house in the prestigious area, the good vacations, the boat. I thought then, and I think now, that if you'd asked her children (or the children of the woman whose kids distracted her), they might want to see a little more of their parents.

In some families, both parents do have to work, just to keep their heads above water; and there are lots of people absolutely entitled to subsidized daycare. None of this is meant as an argument against improving the quality of daycare centers or training for nannies. But there are among the people I work with and interview, a growing number of folks who see nothing contradictory about spending $600 for a suit (and call it "investment dressing") rather than spending $600 worth of their time with their children (which is, surely, a better investment).

Time: not "quality" time, or special "scheduled" time. Just plain old time, and lots of it. Getting the pros to do it for you — whether it's daycare, a nanny, or someone's granny down the street — is unlikely to pay equivalent dividends.

PART FIVE: Friendly Fire

The Band of Brothers

Of all the feminist claptrap of recent years, none is more irritating to me than the smug assertion that women have friendships that are finer, deeper, and altogether superior to those between men, those shallow, towel-flicking creatures who never Really Talk.

I have heard this nonsense from women who think nothing of canceling a long-standing lunch date with another woman because a man called. (Yes, this still happens, the difference being that, the woman is likely to say, "Sara and I are so close, I *know* she won't mind.") I have heard it from women who believe that shopping with their friends is a form of "bonding". I have even heard it from men who have been told so often that they are lousy communicators that they have begun to believe it. And I have read it — in women's magazines, in men's magazines, and in the so-called lifestyle sections of newspapers.

Now, women can have marvelous relationships; I have had a few of these myself, some of which, luckily, I continue to enjoy. They can also have appalling relationships (and I've had a few of those, too), though you rarely hear about them these days.

So big deal: None of this is new, or news. What is new is the attempt to glorify female friendships, simultaneously demeaning male ones, purely on the basis that women talk more and about more intimate matters. I think women do talk more, and they do talk more intimately. But telling another woman that your period is extra heavy this month, or that Michael is terrible in bed, or that you had an abortion does not a friendship make. If it did, women would be bosom buddies with everyone they ever met in a loo. Nor do such confessions automatically elevate a friendship to a higher plane.

The truth, of course, is that men have entirely different sorts of relationships than women do and trying to compare them is futile. Generally, men don't go on about how they feel; women interpret that as not caring how the other guy feels. Generally, men don't touch in the ways that women do — a kiss on the cheek, a hug. Their physical contact tends to be in the form of play or roughhousing; women interpret that as immature and unimportant. Generally, too, men tend to do things with their friends — play sports, get drunk together. From girlhood women get together mainly to talk; they interpret "doing" as superficial.

I spent a good part of my life in hockey arenas, watching boys, and later men, at play. My own father was articulate about his deep love for men he fought beside during the war or played football with. My husband, at the age of thirty, is still playing hockey for fun, and making friends that way. So I think I understand better than many women the lovely and magical friendships that can exist between men.

I am thinking particularly of the weekend hockey tournament David's team plays every spring in a small Muskoka town north of Toronto. On the face of it, with players and a handful of spouses booked into the same hotel, the tournaments are a combination of hockey and partying and some good hard drinking. But there are other things, too: the way the men gently watched over one young fellow who drank too much and not well, until they tucked him safely into bed; their concern for a player who alternated between bouts of manic glee and serious depression; their unspoken agreement to include in every activity the two or three natural "outsiders" in the club; their choice as Most Valuable Player a legitimate candidate for the award who was also the oldest player on the team. He was so touched by and appreciative of their thoughtfulness, his eyes promptly filled with tears.

I remember, too, when one of my husband's friends broke up with his girlfriend of long-standing. Ted would come over often to visit David, and they would talk relentlessly about the National Hockey League playoffs, or the brand-new baseball season or politics (almost everything but what was on his friend's mind). Yet David would never be fooled, and would always know how Ted felt. I'd come home, and ask him how Teddy was, and he'd say, "He's really lonely." "What did he say? Did he talk about it?" "Not much," David would say. "He just said, once, that she was a great woman. I think he's really hurting and it's hit home that it's over." And that night, sure as God made little green apples, David would have invited Teddy for dinner.

Once, a long time ago, I was the only woman at one of those all-male banquets; the occasion was a fundraiser (thus my presence as a sportswriter), and the place was filled with former professional football players who had won Grey Cups together. Much of the night was devoted to serious drinking; but at the end, some of the former players gathered at a bar owned by one of their members. They sat in small groups, cuffing each other on the head, telling lies, occasionally dancing together to the old jukebox or doing handstands, sharing their memories of that violent game, and being friends the way that only men on teams can be friends. Even I, with my sports background and much-cultivated jolly jockdom, felt like a voyeur, albeit privileged to see so close-up the strange bonds between these men.

I found it so moving that I wrote a column about it in the *Globe*. Months later, I got a note from one of the men, still an executive in the Canadian Football League, telling me that I had understood. That column began with a quote from *Henry V*. My Dad quoted it when he talked about his friends in the war, those who were lost and those who survived, men who, fifty years later, still had a lock on his heart:

We few, we happy few, we band of brothers;
For he to-day that sheds his blood with me
Shall be my brother.

You don't have to understand the bond between men to appreciate it. All you have to do is look, and with a reasonably open mind and a heart that hasn't turned to stone, you can see that it is as good and true as any forged between women.

Next-door Neighbors

Once upon a time, your neighbors were also likely to be your friends: You depended on them, particularly if you lived in the country, your children probably played together, you patronized the same stores, and you probably saw them several times a day.

In small towns, people may still live in one another's pockets; but most of us urban creatures are likely to meet our neighbors not the day we move into the area, but the day we prepare to move out. Only when you put the Open House sign on the lawn are you finally guaranteed to meet everyone on your street.

Those of us who live in high-rise apartment buildings may never see the people living next door, or at most, exchange only cursory hellos at the lobby mailboxes. Why, after a crime in a large apartment building, do the police express surprise that no one reported seeing "a stranger" or "a suspicious-looking character". We all know that everyone is a stranger, many are suspicious-looking, and we would never report them to the authorities because they may live down the hall. Modern suburbanites may meet their neighbors by accident, by making the perfectly natural mistake of thinking the four-bedroom, center-hall, brick-front house at 42 Flamingo Way is their four-bedroom, center-hall, brick-front house at 44 Flamingo Way. Those of us who live in established old neighborhoods take special pains — high-privacy fences and enclosed decks — to make sure we never catch a glimpse of the folks next door.

By and large, the day of the friendly neighbor is gone; yet, we are usually forced to have some relationship with our neighbors, because, like Everest, they are there.

Our three-story slum in downtown Toronto is the middle rowhouse in a series of three; so we quickly became uncomfortably aware of our neighbors. On one side, on the third floor, a music teacher gives voice lessons. We memorized his three favorite songs and, I might add, sing them better than 95 percent of his students. On the other side, also on the third floor, is an especially quarrelsome family consisting of a man and woman, their nine- or ten-year-old daughter, and an infant son named Blue. We figure the parents spend so much time staring into Labatt's it's the only color they know.

Well, last Christmas, David and I arose at an ungodly early hour. David still gets so excited about Christmas he can't sleep past six o'clock, and we were going to open up our stockings in bed before heading off to my mother's for the traditional breakfast and tree. We were in the kitchen, grabbing a coffee, when we heard the woman next door:

"You think you're so fucking shit-hot, you and your big cock, well you're shit, that's what you are, you're shit."

Now, this was standard conversation for the woman, as was the grunt from her husband, and the wails of poor Blue. (The little girl, presumably inured to this awfulness, never bothered to cry any more.) But it was particularly loathsome on an otherwise peaceful, still Christmas morning — the street outside dark and snowy, the sky still black. We felt, as always, both enraged and helpless; it never seemed to come to physical violence, the mere hint of which would have had us phoning the Children's Aid or the police; but it was surely emotional abuse, and must have been hell on the children. But on Christmas, Blue and his sister should have been opening gifts, eating oranges, talking excitedly about Santa Claus. Instead, they were forced to listen to the vileness of their parents. And there we were, on the other side of the wall, painfully aware that you cannot phone the police to break up a war of words.

We rarely saw these neighbors; we caught glimpses of the woman hanging from her living-room window, tossing down a key so the girl could come in; occasionally we saw the little one head off to school, her breakfast (a bag of chips) in her hand; the man's big meaty back was silhouetted once in a while in the window. We saw nothing of the little boy, Blue, who never seemed to leave the apartment. But we knew that the woman had an evil, hurtful mouth on her, that her husband and his friends spent most afternoons drinking beer and watching TV, that the girl was shy and nervous and pale, and that Blue was a good baby, who cried only when they fought.

We determined two things. First, our relationship with them would be a careful one: when he played his stereo at full volume, which he did day in and day out, we would not complain and incur his wrath; instead we would soundproof that wall. Second, we would be watchful. If we ever, ever had the slightest inkling that either one of them was laying a hand on one of those kids, we would call in every authority we could find.

The other thing we decided — curious, because we knew them best through the wall; voyeurs drawn to it by what we heard or repelled and driven to another room — was that sometimes, even a little familiarity can breed a lot of contempt.

The Myth of Platonic Friendship

It is not impossible for a man and woman to love each other, as we used to say as teenagers, Like A Friend. But let's face it, there is an element of improbability to the idea. As anyone who ever discouraged a would-be suitor knows full well there is something false about telling someone you love them Like A Friend when, in most cases, you mean there is no physical chemistry. (Maybe we should have said, "But Doug, I do like you . . . Like A Eunuch.")

But we're all adults, and adults can have perfectly wonderful, non-sexual relationships with other adults of the opposite sex.

I believe that.

I also believe it doesn't happen very often. I know several women who claim, "Oh, my best friends are all men". They spend hours on their makeup before seeing these men friends, and then flirt outrageously, engage in such innocently provocative activities as making angels in the snow, ask them to dance to the slow songs, and drive the men's wives to distraction. I know a couple of men who claimed "She and I are Just Friends", who now live in blissful, decidedly unplatonic sin with said women.

It is my contention that in just about every so-called platonic friendship, one party is just pretending, and has a heart and a pair of jeans filled with lust.

I may be wrong — everyone I know swears I am. Maybe I am just a mean-minded suspicious broad. I still say, some men and women should not even attempt a platonic relationship.

In one such category are ex-lovers. It is a rule that people who have been naked together, even once, cannot be platonic friends, and are lying through their teeth if they say they can.

Nor can people be platonic friends who have *never* been naked together. You don't believe me? Just try leaving one of each sex alone in a small room for a few hours. See what happens.

So, disqualify the men you have been naked with and the ones you haven't been naked with, and those left over are the ones with whom you can safely have a platonic relationship and Like As Friends.

The Litany of Losers

She's your friend. She has always been there when you've needed a shoulder to cry on. When you've been drunk and disorderly, she's taken you home, hosed you down, and tucked you in. You have vacationed together, got in trouble together, partied together, bitched about your bosses, maybe even lusted after the same man. The two of you are solid.

And then what happens? Your wonderful friend, your beloved pal falls for a schnook unworthy of licking her boots, a total nerd. Suddenly, she is spending all her time with this hapless swine. On the rare occasions when they are not doing whatever it is they do (you shudder to think), and she is available to see you, she insists on bringing him along. You want to be her friend; you cannot abide him. What do you do?

My dearest friend went through a difficult period a few years back. She adored not one of these hopeless creatures, but a series of them, each more hideous than the last.

The first was Lou. She met Lou at a Hallowe'en party. He was in costume, she thought. (Hell, David and I were there too, and we thought the same thing.) She found him quite fetching. Weeks later, when it turned out he always dressed in cowboy clothes, complete with bandanna at the neck, she became less enchanted. When it also turned out that he had a habit of falling to one knee and proclaiming her beauty in a loud voice, she was plain embarrassed. Finally, she sent him riding off into the sunset, alone.

The second of the Litany of Losers was Andrew, a balding, elongated duck, with an Adam's apple the size of Prince Edward Island. She thought Andrew was the cat's ass. The four of us regularly went out together trying to find a topic about which Andrew had an opinion other than, "Me, too". One day, Andrew simply stopped calling. My friend was quite crushed, but David and I believe he probably just forgot her number.

Mind you, compared to Nick, who came next, he was an intellectual giant. Nick was a good-looking young man who was always on a diet. Nick never ate. He had cigarettes for breakfast, snacks, lunch, and dinner; for an hors d'oeuvre, he'd break down and have a foul-smelling Colt. Nick had a fast, low-slung car; at the slightest sign of a stone in the road, he'd whip out a giant protective bra and hook it over the front grille. He liked disco music; he liked speedboats; he liked cigarettes. You could have a better conversation with a cigarette than you could with Nick.

Then came Chris, a dowdy, overweight fellow who won over my friend by flattering her; then Ali, a middle-aged gentleman who claimed to be a Saudi prince. He was the most vicious racist I ever met, and was prone — perhaps it was the revenge of the god of multiculturalism — to strange physical problems: a twitching eye, piercing headaches, and a shoulder that regularly fell out of its socket. Oh, and Nat, a slick legal eagle who turned out to be a slick, legally married eagle.

On and on it went, the Litany of Losers. None of these

relationships lasted any time, but all of them were terribly important at the moment. David and I tried to cajole her out of seeing some of these guys, teased her about others, but bore with them all.

What else can you do? When your friend is enchanted by a troll, keep a smile on your face and a lid on your lip. If you're lucky, it won't last. If you're not, and it does, at least you'll still have your friend.

Auld Lang Syne

Assuming you are neither a Fag Hag nor a homophobe, the odds are that in your circle of friends, there will be at least one homosexual male.

In ordinary times, the sexual orientation of one's friends is of no consequence; these, however, are not ordinary times. Not for gay men — particularly not for urban gay men, whose ranks have been tragically thinned by AIDS. Even those gay men who have escaped AIDS — your gay friends who are physically healthy and not at great risk — have suffered, and are suffering, some emotional trauma.

One day, a gay friend was feeling overcome with relief. He had just returned from a visit to his doctor to have a curious skin rash checked out. The doctor's diagnosis of garden-variety psoriasis left Alex shaking with gratitude. "I thought," he said, "it might be AIDS."

I was a little surprised, and said so. Alex is young enough to have missed the free love days of the sixties; he came out of the closet late enough that the salad days of Gay Liberation in the seventies all but passed him by. As far as I knew, he was a man who is involved in monogamous, long-term relationships.

"Every gay man I know freaks out about this kind of thing all the time," Alex said. "A bump on your arm, a little spot on your back — anything like that. And we're scared to death to go to the doctor because of what he might tell us. We make ourselves crazy, looking for spots and rashes."

He told me other ways that the lives of ordinary gay men have been changed by AIDS: gay couples in their early thirties, who are "buying a house now," a decade before they'd planned to, "because they don't know how long they'll be around"; young gay men who have made their wills, which they never would have done pre-AIDS.

"And then," he said, "there are our little suicide pacts." Seeing the shock on my face, he explained. "Not suicide pacts really, but death pacts." Two or three close friends pledge that, if one of them is "diagnosed" (the euphemism for being told you have AIDS; thereafter, everything revolves around "how long you've been diagnosed"), the others will help as long as they can; but when the patient is terribly ill and suffering, they will see to it that he has access to a bottle of sleeping pills or other means to take his own life. "Everyone I know has made some kind of arrangement like this," Alex said. "We've all seen someone die that awful, slow, painful death. We don't want to die like that."

It isn't only People With AIDS who are hurting. It isn't just that practically every young urban gay man has gone to more than his share of funerals. It isn't merely that the bars, the discos, the casual sex that was, at least in part, a proclamation of gay pride and freedom have been closed down.

AIDS is, as much as anything, about fear; its dreadful specter has irrevocably altered the lives of gay men in ways that undermine self-confidence and destroy the small joys and the freedoms the straight world still takes for granted: when a heterosexual sees a rash on his chest, he assumes it is an allergy; gay men think of AIDS.

There isn't much you can do, perhaps, except to know that your friend is probably afraid, that real or not, he senses the shadow of death. If that knowledge does nothing more than make you a little more aware, a little more compassionate, and a little more understanding of the gay men's sense of loss, of longing for auld lang syne, when the young did not make death pacts, it has helped.

The Difference Between Mothers and Friends

The latest fashionable belief from the eighties school of Superior Female Friendships holds that mothers and daughters can become Best Friends. The women's magazines are full of testimonials, moving tales of mothers and daughters who, after the normal years of quarreling are past, find themselves equals, linking arms and striding together down the road to real friendship.

To this, I say, Ha! Fat chance!

I love my mother, always have, always will. I confess that once my teenage years — the era of door-slamming and tears — were over, we immediately began to get along better; I further acknowledge that once I moved out on my own, we got along even better. I'll even grudgingly admit that once I was safely married, we might even have appeared to the world at large to be happy equals. But there is no way on God's green earth that we will ever be Best Friends.

For one thing, mothers and daughters can never be equals: the old one is always first and foremost, the mother; the younger one remains the one the mother bossed around. You do not shake the habits of a lifetime ("Where are your mitts? Why are you wearing that dress? Off the phone! Go to your room until you decide you can behave nicely! You're wearing too much makeup! You're grounded!") merely because your daughter has attained the age of majority, or has seven children, and gray hair. Age — of daughter or mother — has nothing to do with it.

Another thing: Being Best Friends with someone means that the two of you confess to each other: your deepest insecurities, your sexual adventures, your youthful experiments with drugs. Perhaps there are some mothers who would not blanch visibly at this sort of intimacy, but mine would.

My mother nearly walked out of *An Officer and a Gentleman,* she was so unnerved by the explicit sex scenes. (She vowed never to see another movie, and as far as I know, has kept her promise.) Not only was she pissed off with "that nice Debra Winger" for taking off her clothes "well, like *that*", she was also annoyed with me, and all I did was take her to the damn movie. Can you imagine how she'd react if she learned I'd behaved like Debra Winger? (Not, Ma, that I ever have, heh, heh.)

The very idea of telling my mother my darkest insecurities is frightening. Without me saying a word, she knows some of them and, during a quarrel, heads directly for them, without passing GO. ("But honey, your black dress makes you look so much slimmer." or "Aren't you getting a little long in the tooth for mini-skirts?") Am I going to tell this woman, voluntarily, that I think my ankles are fat and my lips too thin? Am I crazy?

Finally, what precludes a mother-daughter friendship is that in gaining a friend, one would lose a mother. Frankly, I would rather keep mine. I have friends; I have one mother.

When those women in the magazines ("My mother, my friend") have a nasty cold, where do they turn for advice and homemade soup? When they want to feel stupidly safe and protected, to whose house do they go? And when, as surely they must, they break into odd bits of song whilst housecleaning ("Three little fishies and the momma fishy, too, and they swam and they swam all over the dam" or "Be kind to your web-footed friends, for a duck may be somebody's brother. . . . He lives in a place called a swamp, where it's always cold and damp"), and are caught in the act by their husbands, what do they say? Do they say, "Oh, that's a silly song my Best Friend taught me?" Give me a break: The only people who know those songs are mothers, and the only people they teach them to are daughters. T'was ever thus, and so it should remain.

How to Keep Friends and Influence No One

I once had a conversation with a friend of mine that went something like this:

Her: "If you ever find out that Bob is fooling around on me, I want you to tell me."

Me: "Oh, I will."

Her: "No, I mean it, I'd want to know. I'd *hate* to be the last one to know. I want you to tell me"

Me: "Oh, I will, I promise."

I lied. I wouldn't, and I won't. Honesty is a much overrated virtue, especially between friends. Besides, in really delicate matters, someone else will take pains to break the bad news and enlighten your friend. You emerge unscathed and will not be in danger of being the messenger who is shot.

Five things women should never tell a friend:

1. that she is too fat for a bikini. (Her mother will tell her.)
2. that her husband is having an affair. (Someone in his office will tell her.)
3. that her roots are showing. (Mother again.)
4. that her teenage daughter is pregnant. (No one will tell her; but one day, she will ask the daughter if she is putting on weight. The daughter will burst into tears.)

5. that her son is into drugs. (The police will tell her.)

Five things men should never tell a friend:

1. that he is losing his hair. (His father will tell him.)
2. that he is not as fast on the blades as he used to be. (The young snot on the team will tell him.)
3. that X at the office is making more money than he is. (X will tell him.)
4. that his teenager daughter is pregnant. (His wife, having guessed, will tell him.)
5. that his paunch makes him look pregnant. (His daughter, who is pregnant, will tell him.)

Stick to these guidelines, and it is unlikely a friend will attempt to punch out your lights.

Looking for Mr. (and Mrs.) Goodbar

Sometimes, it seems the entire world was designed by Noah. First we are expected to find one of our species and form a couple; then we are expected to find other couples with whom to be compatible. Anyone who has been trapped in a small cottage on a rainy weekend with her spouse and another couple (one of whom was wonderful, the other a whiner who refuses to do a lick of work) knows all too well that if the search for Mr. Goodbar is tricky, tracking down Mr. and Mrs. Goodbar can be a real bitch.

I can't remember the number of times that David and I, after spending an evening with another couple, agreed afterwards that X was terrific company, and Y was a bore. (I sense that in the other couple's similar discussions of us David was X and I was Y, but what the hell.) It always happens: You like him, but despise her. Your spouse likes her, but deems him pompous and overbearing. Both of you adore one party and abhor the other. How are couples, married or not, ever going to find people to play cards with, go dancing with, or invite over for dinner?

The answer, of course, is either through their children, or the grace of God.

If your children get along with their children, the odds are that you will also get along with them. Also, by seeing the other couple first as parents, you can learn much about them: a little of their values (Do they make little Peggy take back the chocolate bar she stole from Food City, or do they forget it ever happened?); how they behave under stress (What happens when your Johnny has beaten the pants off Peggy — or worse, taken off her pants to examine what was in them?); and, perhaps most important, what kind of food they eat (When Peggy eats over at your house, does she crave miniature marshmallows and canned soup?).

Children are not born liking plastic food. If they like it, it's because they're fed it every Friday. (This may not preclude your making friends with the child's parents, but should you be invited over for supper, you will be forewarned.) Similarly, children do not occur naturally as pale, unhappy, red-eyed creatures; but you should not be surprised to discover that Mom and Dad are pale, unhappy, red-eyed adults, and that you and yours may not want to go away camping with them.

If you do not have children or if your children are teenagers (in which case, you will not know their friends, let alone if they have parents), you will be on your own — without benefit of the child-icebreaker.

In this case, all you can do is be alert for signs of trouble, for two persons who are unhappy with each other are unlikely to be splendid company for anyone else, even if separately they are utterly adorable. The man and woman who indulge in nasty, highly personal public quarrels (wherein he "teases" her about the size of her breasts and she makes "jokes" about him having trouble getting it up) are trouble. So is the couple that is overly affectionate in public. (I have long believed that after the honeymoon stage, the husband and wife who are all over each other in a crowd probably ignore each other in their bedroom.) Also, any two adults who address each other as "Sweetchips" and "Pookie" are unlikely to make interesting dinner companions. Ditto for any pair who feed bits of their meal to the other.

Mostly, however, it's a matter of luck. But even when you've found a wonderful couple to befriend, it may not last. David and I found such a pair once: We loved him; we loved her. He was quiet, but not a mouse; she was gregarious, but not loud. The four of us hit it off immediately, and within weeks of meeting were having immensely enjoyable dinners-cum-all-night-card-games.

Alas, we liked them more than they liked each other. Within three months, they had broken up, and we were back on Noah's Ark, feeling like the only two zebras aboard.

Rites of Passage

An accurate measure of how old you are (as opposed to how old you feel, how old you would like to be, or how old you think you look) is the sort of surprise party your friends are planning for you — or would be, were they so inclined. Such entertainment is the only real down side to friends; some of whom regard it as a serious obligation. If your friends are among them, you may be doomed to any number of these painful events.

The first social surprise is the wedding shower or stag. Both require that you behave in a manner altogether foreign to your nature. At the former, you must show great excitement over oven mitts, pot holders, coordinated napkin-and-placemat sets and toaster ovens. At the latter, you are obliged to drink heavily, play cards all night, watch cheap films featuring naked women and large dogs, and be forcibly beaten about the face and head by a set of professional breasts hired expressly for your amusement.

Both events may also be surprises, in which case you must act delighted and surprised. Even if the event is a genuine surprise, you will have trouble. Most people faced with a surprise find it extremely difficult to behave in a manner recognizable as surprise. Raised eyebrows and small, pleased smiles come easily to few of us and occur naturally only on television. Real-life surprise usually looks a lot like horror.

(Incidentally, one side-effect of feminism is the surprise "stag" for the bride, instead of a shower. This is regrettable. It may be difficult to feign delight whilst wearing a paper plate covered with bows and eating crustless sandwiches, but it is infinitely more difficult whilst a near-naked stranger is hefting his parts only inches from your face.)

The second event at which the honor of your surprise may be requested is the baby shower. You will be expected to coo, fuss, and get all weepy at the sight of miniature garments, rubber duckies, and giant boxes of Pampers. Fortunately, the nature of the event and hormones both come into play, and you will likely oblige your hosts with happy tears.

The most dreaded on the list are surprise birthday parties, usually commemorating a Big Birthday — your thirtieth or fortieth or fiftieth. These are not really Big birthdays, they are Old birthdays. Though your friends may be roughly your age, and despise the idea of anyone throwing them such a party, they will think nothing of doing so for you.

The last sort of surprise party at which you could be humiliated is the anniversary party, celebrating your golden, silver, bronze, or runners-up wedding anniversary. I know whereof I speak on this one because I once organized such a fête for my parents. In a moment of foolishness, I talked myself into thinking that my parents would be pleased to be surprised on their forty-fifth anniversary (and perhaps, in theory, they were). My Dad was also very ill, and I knew he would not be around for his fiftieth.

We lured them to a friend's house on the old pretext of dinner, and they were, I think, duly surprised. I doubt either of them had any idea what was in store. However, I will always remember the look of horror on my father's face when he walked into that room to see fifty or so of their friends. He was glad to see them, you understand, and I believe he was touched by the gesture; but he was also embarrassed, because he was sick and thin, and, of course, because he was the center of attention. I, too, would have been mortified in his place. The road of good intentions is paved with an awful lot of silly mistakes, and if I'd thought less about how the party would make me look (The Good Daughter) and more about how it would make him feel (The Old Fart), I would never have done it.

He knew, as did I, albeit belatedly, that the anniversary party is a precursor of the funeral.

It is, in other words, enough that you are aware of how old you are, of what rite of passage you are undergoing. You do not need public reminders, no matter how well-meaning. If anyone ever throws a surprise party for me, I will not look pleased. I will not look surprised. I will leave town.

Dogs and Books

At some of the lowest moments of my life, in my times of worst despair, I have depended on two categories of friends to pull me through, and neither has ever let me down. One is books; the other is dogs.

This is not meant to disparage my human friends, some of whom I have relied on heavily, all of whom I love. But, as we all learn sooner or later, people can't always be with you when you need them. Sometimes, they mean to say the right thing, the comforting thing, but they say the wrong one.

Other times, they have problems of their own and cannot be strong for you. Even when they are there, to hold your hand and kiss it better, they cannot take away the source of your unhappiness.

Books can. And so can dogs.

Books are the ultimate escape. When my heart has been broken, when I worry about my job or my writing, when I feel let down, betrayed, or unloved, I read a book. As a young woman in search of romance, I read, oddly enough, John D. MacDonald's Travis McGee books. When no one else was there to play the part, Travis was my white knight, a man both rough and tender, who loved both his friends and a woman who was loyal and sexy, fierce and faithful.

When my dad was in hospital and I was frantic he would never, ever get out, I could lose myself only when I read. I read everything, anytime — in the bathroom, on the subway, waiting for a bus, and every night before I fell asleep. And when my father went into hospital for the last time, and when he died, I cried and cried, and then remembered and remembered. The only thing that could stop the tears and the memories was reading. Much later, when I feared he was slipping away from my memory, I could bring him back, as sharp as daylight, by reading the book of Edna St. Vincent Millay's poetry he'd given me, or Kipling's *The Jungle Book* that he used to read to me as a child, or one of his favorite novels.

Not throughout my life, but for periods of it, the other source of comfort and love was my dog. As a pudgy young girl with all the usual insecurities, I came home from school every day to the wholehearted adoration of Lucky, a big, ham-footed, foolish boxer. As a shy, easily embarrassed (and thus perfectly normal) teenager, it was sweet Mickey who welcomed me. As a reasonably young adult, I looked to wondrous, even-tempered, overtly affectionate Susie. And now, as a fairly well-adjusted, usually happy adult, I have Blux, the big black half-Labrador with paws like hamburger buns and a heart the size of his geographic name.

It is trite to say that dogs love you no matter what; but they do, and there are times when the human being craves undemanding, uncritical, and wholly accepting love. If you're lucky, you get it as a child, from your parents; but as you become an adult you lose the right to remain uncriticized. They may love you anyway, but they are likely to explain that anyway at great and painful length. You can ignore a dog, leave him unattended and unwalked for far too long; yet the minute you walk through the door, he will be all over you like a cheap suit. You can be mean to a dog, and he will forgive you; what's more, he will never remember your meanness, let alone extract vengeance. When you want to play, so will he; when you need hugging, he will, too. When you crave quiet, pleasant company, that's just what he'll give you; when nothing and no one can make you laugh, he can reduce you to stupid, teary howling within seconds. When everyone you know is busy or in love or on vacation or booked up, it will be his distinct pleasure to be available.

Dogs are individuals as much as people are, but all dogs that are treated well share some delightful characteristics: loyalty, generosity, and a temperament that is warm and loving. And though it is silly to imbue them with human characteristics or understanding, they are none the less bright, inquisitive creatures who can immensely enrich your life. Also, they are worthy of love. Probably, there are some nice people around who happen not to like dogs, but I'll be damned if I can think of any.

I remember a friend whose three-year relationship abruptly ended. Suddenly, he was cut off from everything familiar — the woman he still loved, the house they had worked on together, the bed he knew, the street he was fond of, neighbors he knew, flowers he had planted. When he left, all he took were his clothes and a small knapsack of personal treasures.

He moved into a stark, modern apartment; he had virtually no furniture but cardboard boxes. David and I lived nearby, and saw him frequently in those days; and many times, when he thought no one would notice, I caught him looking with incredible love and gratitude at a large tan-and-white object on the floor beside him.

His dog was the one familiar, beloved face in his brave new world. He was properly appreciative, and respectful, and enamored of her for simply being with him. And later, when his life straightened out, as it usually does for good people, and there was a new woman to share things with, he never forgot what his hound had meant to him in the dark days. You stick with them what brung you, my daddy always said. And nine times out of ten, that's a hound.

Now, if only I could find a dog who'd read out loud to me: a jug of wine, a book to read, a dog beside me panting in the sun, tail wagging in slow motion in the heat. Well, that's heaven.